All You Need is Good News
Paul's letter to Rome

Doug Rowston

Published by
GRACE & PEACE BOOKS
4A Wurilba Ave Hawthorn SA 5062 Australia

djrowston@gmail.com
© 2022 Douglas James Rowston

All rights reserved. This publication is copyright. Photographs were taken by the author. Other than for the purposes of and subject to the conditions of the Copyright Act, no part of it may in any form or by any means (electronic, mechanical, microcopying, photocopying, recording or otherwise) be reproduced, stored in a retrieval system or transmitted without prior written permission from the publisher.

Published 2023 ISBN 978-0-6453288-7-5

Acknowledgements

Bible quotations are from the New Revised Standard Version Bible, Anglicized Edition, copyright © 1989, 1995 by the Division of Christian Education of the National Council of Churches of Christ in the U S A. Used by permission. All rights reserved.

The front cover features a statue of Caesar Augustus in Rome.

This book is dedicated to

Alan McKee

ADVANCE REVIEWS

Doug Rowston is an enthusiastic student and teacher of Christian Scripture for individuals and groups. In this his eighth book, *All You Need is Good News: Paul's letter to Rome*, he has combined a great balance of the English text with analysis of the message for both then and now, providing both a prayer and searching questions for each section, plus plenty of references to further resources. As in other books he has used photographs effectively to enhance understanding, these from his own travels to Rome and surrounding areas.

A provocative feature is also the accounts of the impact of Romans on five significant men from various periods of history: Aurelius Augustine (354-430), Martin Luther (1489-1546), John Wesley (1703-1791), Karl Barth (1886-1968), and David Suchet (1946-). (My only wish is that he had found a female example!)

Doug concludes this book confidently: "When we read Paul's greatest letter with heart and mind, God our Father is able to keep filling us with joy and peace that comes from trusting in his Son Jesus, with the result that we overflow with hope by the Holy Spirit despite the ups and downs of life." I am confident that this book will provide readers with tools the Spirit can use for their joy and peace and hope in a changing world.

Dr Rosalind Gooden
Former ABMS Missionary in Bangladesh

Doug Rowston is indeed right to quote Dale Moody's reflection that 'the well of Romans was too deep to run dry' –and Rowston's engaging handling of this profound text illustrates the truth of that observation. With commendably concise prose, this treatment balances concern for the overarching narrative and development of Paul's argument, alongside identifying and providing helpful guidance in exploring the multifaceted pathways and directions that comprise this rich text.

Creatively employing a framework of Tragedy, Comedy, Dilemma and Fairy Tale, Rowston succeeds in capturing something of the performative quality of a text that was written to be 'performed' (read aloud) when presented to the original recipients. Woven through this analysis are a selection of vignettes of lives touched by Romans from a variety of contexts and times. Through this interplay Rowston brings to the fore an even greater quality evident in Paul's letter – that this is no mere document of passing interest to ancient historians but is truly God-breathed and continues to speak as such as God's living word.

Writing such an overview, summary and guide for Romans is deceptively challenging. All too many read into the text more than is there or provide cursory summations that reflect more the views of the commentator than the theological and pastoral richness found in Paul's own words. Rowston's treatment reflects the maturity of someone who has lived in ongoing reflection and learning, combining the eyes of a disciple, pastor and theological educator.

Any treatment of Romans should lead us to two indispensable landing points: to prayer and praise! It is a pleasure to see these qualities embodied in this stimulating and helpful book.

Dr Tim Harris
Assistant Bishop, Anglican Diocese of Adelaide

Filled with details gathered from a lifetime of study, Doug Rowston is a well-informed guide who wants to encourage his readers – both individuals and small groups – towards a devotional (and life-shaping) encounter with the good news of Jesus found in Paul's letter to the Romans.

The letter is explored within a creative four-part structure of 'sad news' (Romans 1:18- 3:20), 'glad news' (Romans 3:21-8:39), a gospel that engages dilemmas of past, present, and future (Romans 9:1-11:36), and 'too good not to be true!' news (Romans 12:1-15:13).

In seventeen bite-sized sections, Paul's thought is explored through commentary, stories, thought-provoking questions, and prayers. Identifying Romans as a letter that has "influenced the world very significantly," brief accounts are included of five historical characters who have been transformed by their reading of Romans in the hope that contemporary readers will also be stimulated to deeds of faith, hope, and love.

This is a gentle study that shows evidence of Doug's extensive experience as a patient teacher and preacher.

Dr Stephen Spence
Author, *The Parting of the Ways*

CONTENTS

Foreword   1

Introduction
Why should we read Romans?   3
A Personal Pilgrimage with Romans   5
The Gospel of God   7
The Background of Paul's Letter to Rome   9
An Overview of Paul's Letter to Rome   13
An Outline of Paul's Letter to Rome   15

The Opening of the Letter
Romans 1:1-17 Greeting, Thanksgiving, Theme   17
Aurelius Augustine's Story   20

First Major Section
Tragedy: How is Romans sad news to Gentiles and Jews?

Romans 1:18-32	In the Gentile world	21
Romans 2:1-3:8	In the Jewish world	25
Romans 3:9-20	In all the world	31
Martin Luther's Story		33

Second Major Section
Comedy: How is Romans glad news to all who believe?

Romans 3:21-31	In Jesus Christ	35
Romans 4:1-25	In Abraham	39
Romans 5:1-21	In grace	43
Romans 6:1-23	In eternal life	47
Romans 7:1-25	In liberation	53
Romans 8:1-39	In the Spirit	57
John Wesley's Story		65

Third Major Section
Dilemma: How is Romans good news to Jew and Gentile?
Romans 9:1-29   Past tragedy   67
Romans 9:30-10:21   Present responsibility   73
Romans 11:1-36   Future mystery   79
Karl Barth's Story   85

Fourth Major Section
Fairy Tale: How is Romans news too good not to be true?
Romans 12:1-21   The upward relation   87
Romans 13:1-14   The outward relation   93
Romans 14:1-15:13   The inward relation   97
David Suchet's Story   103

The Closing of the Letter
Romans 15:14-16:27   Plans, Greetings, Praise   105

Appendix: The God of Jesus and Paul   111

Afterword   115

Select Bibliography   117

Foreword

On July 23, 2020, the second last day of a delightful holiday with my wife at Robe in South Australia, I had a significant heart attack. In the providence of God the doctor at the Robe Medical Centre stabilised me and I was transported to Flinders Private Hospital by road ambulance and flying doctor service. All the way the doctors and nurses and paramedics were truly amazing. While Rosalie was driving home alone I was being cared for in Adelaide. The cardiologist planned my treatment. This included an emergency operation on July 25 for the insertion of a stent, time at home for healing and gathering strength before readmission to hospital, and triple bypass surgery on September 15. In retrospect I can only think of a verse in the New Testament. *We know that all things work together for good for those who love God (Romans 8:28).*

More than two years after this experience I have written the following book on Romans, Paul's greatest letter. This is designed to be read by individuals or home groups. Individuals may use it as a collection of devotional studies over an extended time. Home groups may work through a series of weekly or fortnightly gatherings. After the introduction each short section includes the biblical text, some explanatory comments, a prayer, and some questions for discussion. My desire is that readers will come to appreciate the good news that was communicated by Paul in the first century and that still speaks to readers in the twenty-first century. And I trust you, like me, will learn that all things work together for good for those who love God.

Doug Rowston

All You Need is Good News

*Forum
Rome*

Introduction

Why should we read Romans?

This book is about a letter written by a man who lived in the first century of the Christian era. He was named Saul, in Hebrew, or Paul, in Greek. Hebrew was the ancient language of his people, the Jews. Greek was the common language of his world, the Roman Empire. In the second half of the second century, an anonymous writer described Paul as follows: 'a man small of stature, with a bald head and crooked legs, in a good state of body, with eyebrows meeting and nose somewhat hooked, full of friendliness; for now he appeared like a man, and now he had the face of an angel.' Paul's personal appearance is depicted in such a plain and unflattering manner that the description may well reflect the truth.

This man may have had not only an ugly appearance but he also had an ugly beginning in the history of Christianity. He was in favour of stoning a leading Greek-speaking Jewish Christian, Stephen, and he was actively involved in throwing other Greek-speaking Jewish Christians into jail. But then things changed dramatically. On the way to persecute Christians in Damascus, Paul met the risen Jesus. Paul turned from the darkness to the light. He became a Christian. In time, he made three major journeys to share the good news which he had found through faith in Jesus the Messiah. Eventually, he was taken to Rome and was brought to trial before the emperor. Finally, like Stephen, he was prepared to die for his faith.

Why then do people make the effort to study this man's letter to the Romans? A very good reason is that the letter to Rome has influenced the history of the world very significantly. It has changed the lives of some of the world's greatest thinkers. Scattered through this book are the testimonies of some very famous characters in Christian history: Aurelius Augustine (354-430), Martin Luther (1483-1546), John Wesley (1703-1791), Karl Barth (1886-1968), and David Suchet (1946-). The common denominator of these five characters is the transforming power of the message of Paul's letter to the Romans. If it has had such an influence, then it seems a worthwhile exercise to make our way through the sixteen chapters of the letter.

A Personal Pilgrimage with Romans

The year 1968 was the first of three and a half years I studied New Testament in the doctoral programme at Southern Seminary in Louisville, Kentucky. What a year it was! The Vietnam War dragged on, Lyndon Johnson withdrew from the Presidential race, Martin Luther King was killed in April by James Earl Ray, Robert Kennedy was assassinated by Sirhan Sirhan in June, and Richard Nixon was elected President in November by an unwitting American public. In the middle of the year I audited a course of memorable lectures by Dale Moody on Paul's Letter to the Romans. These lectures led to his commentary on Romans in *Broadman Bible Commentary*, published in 1970. Moody, a Texan born in 1915, was a fascinating speaker and a gifted biblical theologian. His classes at Southern Seminary were highly entertaining. His literary heritage includes *Spirit of the Living God* and *The Word of Truth*. He served as Professor of Theology from 1948 to 1984 at Southern Seminary. He died in 1992 and is buried in Cave Hill Cemetery, Louisville. Moody wrote truly in his commentary: 'There will never be a definitive commentary on Romans, for the well is too deep to run dry, so all may still come to this fountain to renew faith.'

Over the intervening years I have taught students in classes, preached to church congregations, and led home groups on Romans. There are many useful resources including C. H. Dodd's *Moffatt New Testament Commentary*, C. K. Barrett's *Black New Testament Commentary*, the old *International Critical Commentary* by William Sanday and A. C. Headlam, the new *International Critical Commentary* by Charles Cranfield, the *New Century Bible* by Matthew Black, the full scale works of Ernst Käsemann, Leon Morris, James Dunn, Douglas Moo, Charles Talbert, N. T. Wright, and Ben Witherington. At a popular level, William Barclay in *The Daily Study Bible*, James Dunn in *The People's Bible Commentary*, Fleming Rutledge's sermons on Romans, and Tom Wright in *Paul for Everyone Romans Parts 1 & 2* provide helpful reading for lay people. One volume Bible commentaries have been blessed by the contributions of T. W. Manson in *Peake's Commentary*, Dan Via in *Mercer Commentary*, and John Reumann in *Eerdmans Commentary*. Yes, Dale Moody was correct to say that the well of Romans was too deep to run dry.

The Gospel of God

At the beginning and towards the end of Romans Paul mentions *the gospel of God*.

(1) *gospel* is the translation of the Greek word *euangelion*. The Bauer Lexicon gives three meanings of *euangelion*: '1. God's good news to humans, *good news* as proclamation; 2. details relating to the life and ministry of Jesus, *good news of Jesus*; 3. a book dealing with the life and teaching of Jesus, a *gospel account* that deals with the life and teaching of Jesus.'

In Romans 1:1 and 15:16 the word *gospel* is categorised under meaning 1. In the former, Paul is *a servant of Jesus Christ, called to be an apostle, set apart for the gospel of God*. In the latter, Paul is *a minister of Christ Jesus to the Gentiles in the priestly service of the gospel of God.*

According to the *Macquarie Dictionary*, the English word 'gospel' is Middle English (1100-1500) from Old English (before 1100) *gōd* GOOD + *spell* tidings.

(2) *of God* is the translation of the Greek word *theou*. The Bauer Lexicon gives five meanings of *theos*: '1. In the Greco-Roman world *theos* refers to a transcendent being who exercises extraordinary control in human affairs or is responsible for bestowal of unusual benefits, *deity, god, goddess*. 2. Some writings in the NT use the word with reference to Christ. 3. God in Israelite/Christian monotheistic perspective, *God*. 4. that which is nontranscendent but considered worthy of special reverence or respect, *god*. 5. of the devil, *the god of this age*.'

In Romans 1:1 and 15:16 the word God is best understood as meaning 3. Paul is *set apart for the gospel of God* and *in the priestly service of God* in Israelite/Christian monotheistic perspective.

The Background of Paul's Letter to Rome

Paul is in Corinth about AD 57: *I commend to you our sister Phoebe, a deacon of the church at Cenchreae ... Gaius, who is host to me and to the whole church, greets you. Erastus, the city treasurer, and our brother Quartus, greet you.(16:1, 23)* Paul is writing to Christians in Rome where he has not been. But he has some friends there: *Greet Prisca and Aquila ... Greet also the church in their house. Greet my beloved Epaenetus ... Mary ... Andronicus and Junia ... Greet Ampliatus ... Urbanus ... and my beloved Stachys. Greet Apelles ... those who belong to the family of Aristobulus. Greet my relative Herodion ... those in the Lord who belong to the family of Narcissus ... those workers in the Lord, Tryphaena and Tryphosa ... the beloved Persis ... Rufus ...and ... his mother. Greet Asyncritus, Phlegon, Hermes, Patrobas, Hermas, and the brothers and sisters who are with them ... Philologus, Julia, Nereus and his sister, and Olympas, and all the saints who are with them (16:3-15).*

Paul is taking an offering to help the poor among God's people in Jerusalem: *At present, however, I am going to Jerusalem in a ministry to the saints; for Macedonia and Achaia have been pleased to share their resources with the poor among the saints at Jerusalem (15:25-26).* He is also hoping to conduct a missionary journey after his visit to Jerusalem. He needs the prayers of his readers in view of the perils of the Jerusalem visit. He is aware that he will need to defend himself in Jerusalem: *I appeal to you, brothers and sisters, by our Lord Jesus Christ and by the love of the Spirit, to join me in earnest prayer to God on my behalf, that I may be rescued from the unbelievers in Judea, and that my ministry to Jerusalem may be acceptable to the saints (15:30-31).*

Paul is also aware of the need for unity among the Christians at Rome. There had been an exodus of Jews from the city during the rule of Claudius. Then there had been a return of Jews to Rome after the end of the rule of Claudius. In the meantime Gentile Christians had asserted their leadership of the house churches of Rome. On the return of Jews, Christian and non Christian, relations between Jewish and Gentile Christians will require sensitive and thoughtful negotiations. This is the background of the discussion of the weak and the strong: *Welcome those who are weak in faith, but not for the purpose of quarreling over opinions ... Let us therefore no longer pass judgement on one another, but resolve instead never to put a stumbling block or hindrance in the way of another ... Let us then pursue what makes for peace and for mutual upbuilding (14:1, 13, 19).*

Paul also needs the practical support of the Christians in Rome on his proposal to do missionary work in Spain: *But now, with no further place for me in these regions, I desire, as I have for many years, to come to you when I go to Spain. For I do hope to see you on my journey and to be sent on by you, once I have enjoyed your company for a little while ... So, when I have completed this, and have delivered to them what has been collected, I will set out by way of you to Spain; and I know that when I come to you, I will come in the fullness of the blessing of Christ (15:23, 24, 28, 29).*

In the light of these matters Paul takes the opportunity to share his understanding of the gospel. His letter to Rome is rightfully understood as Christianity according to Paul. Romans has three purposes: a missionary purpose, an apologetic purpose, and a pastoral purpose. Paul is indicating *what* the gospel is that he preaches, *why* as a Jew he preaches the gospel to both Jew and Gentile, and *how* the gospel comes to expression in the life of Christians personally and communally.

All You Need is Good News

*Tribunal
Corinth*

An Overview of Paul's Letter to Rome

Frederick Buechner delivered the Beecher Lectures on preaching at Yale University in 1976. They were published as *Telling the Truth: The Gospel as Tragedy, Comedy, and Fairy Tale* a year later. At the end of the book he sums up his lectures as follows:

'Let the preacher tell the truth. Let him make audible the silence of the news of the world with the sound turned off so that in that silence we can hear the tragic truth of the Gospel, which is that the world where God is absent is a dark and echoing emptiness; and the comic truth of the Gospel, which is that it is into the depths of his absence that God makes himself present in such unlikely ways and to such unlikely people that ... you and I laugh till the tears run down our cheeks. And finally let him preach this overwhelming of tragedy by comedy, of darkness by light, of the ordinary by the extraordinary, as the tale that is too good not to be true because to dismiss it as untrue is to dismiss along with it that catch of the breath, that beat and lifting of the heart near to or even accompanied by tears, which I believe is the deepest intuition of truth that we have.'

Buechner's analysis of preaching is utilised in my treatment to rename three of the four major sections of Romans.

In summary, the Letter to the Romans has an opening (Romans 1:1-17) and a closing (Romans 15:14-16:27). In between are four major sections.

First, *the wrath of God is revealed from heaven against all ungodliness and wickedness* (Romans 1:18-3:20). Paul writes about the **'tragedy'** of the sin of humanity, the sad news.

Second, *the gospel ... is the power of God for salvation to everyone who has faith ... For in it the righteousness of God is revealed through faith for faith* (Romans 3:21-8:39). Paul writes about the **'comedy'** of the grace of God, the glad news.

Third, *the gospel ... is the power of God for salvation to everyone who has faith, to the Jew first and also to the Greek* (Romans 9:1-11:36). Paul deals with the **dilemma** of the purposes of God for Jews and Gentiles.

Fourth, *'The one who is righteous will live by faith'* (Romans 12:1-15:13). Paul writes about the **'fairy tale'** of the Christian life, the news which is too good not to be true.

Prayer

Blessed Lord, you have caused all holy Scriptures to be written for our learning. Grant that we may so hear them, read, mark, learn and inwardly digest them, that, by patience and the comfort of your holy word, we may embrace and ever hold fast the blessed hope of everlasting life, which you have given us in our Saviour Jesus Christ. Amen.

[Thomas Cranmer (1489-1556) revised]

An Outline of Paul's Letter to Rome

Opening

Romans 1:1-17

1:1-7	Greeting
1:8-15	Thanksgiving
1:16-17	Theme

1 Tragedy: How is Paul's letter to the Romans sad news to Gentiles and Jews?

Romans 1:18-3:20

1:18-32	The tragedy of sin in the Gentile world
2:1-3:8	The tragedy of sin in the Jewish world
3:9-20	The tragedy of sin in the whole world

2 Comedy: How is Paul's letter to the Romans glad news to all who believe?

Romans 3:21-8:39

3:21-31	In Jesus Christ: judge, benefactor, priest
4:1-25	In Abraham: father of faithful
5:1-21	In grace instead of wrath
6:1-23	In eternal life instead of sin
7:1-25	In liberation instead of law
8:1-39	In the Spirit instead of death

3 Dilemma: How is Paul's letter to the Romans good news to Jews and Gentiles ?

Romans 9:1-11:36

9:1-29   The dilemma of past tragedy
9:30-10:21   The dilemma of present responsibility
11:1-36   The dilemma of future mystery

4 Fairy Tale: How is Paul's letter to the Romans news too good not to be true?

Romans 12:1-15:13

12:1-21   The fairy tale of the upward relation
13:1-14   The fairy tale of the outward relation
14:1-15:13   The fairy tale of the inward relation

Closing

Romans 15:14-16:27

15:14-33   Plans
16:1-23   Greetings
16:25-27   Praise

The Opening of the Letter

Romans 1:1-17 includes greeting (1:1-7), thanksgiving (1:8-15), theme (1:16-17).

1 Paul, a servant of Jesus Christ, called to be an apostle, set apart for the gospel of God, 2 which he promised beforehand through his prophets in the holy scriptures, 3 the gospel concerning his Son, who was descended from David according to the flesh 4 and was declared to be Son of God with power according to the spirit of holiness by resurrection from the dead, Jesus Christ our Lord, 5 through whom we have received grace and apostleship to bring about the obedience of faith among all the Gentiles for the sake of his name, 6 including yourselves who are called to belong to Jesus Christ, 7 To all God's beloved in Rome, who are called to be saints: Grace to you and peace from God our Father and the Lord Jesus Christ. 8 First, I thank my God through Jesus Christ for all of you, because your faith is proclaimed throughout the world. 9 For God, whom I serve with my spirit by announcing the gospel of his Son, is my witness that without ceasing I remember you always in my prayers, 10 asking that by God's will I may somehow at last succeed in coming to you. 11 For I am longing to see you so that I may share with you some spiritual gift to strengthen you— 12 or rather so that we may be mutually encouraged by each other's faith, both yours and mine. 13 I want you to know, brothers and sisters, that I have often intended to come to you (but thus far have been prevented), in order that I may reap some harvest among you as I have among the rest of the Gentiles. 14 I am a debtor both to Greeks and to barbarians, both to the wise and to the foolish 15 —hence my eagerness to proclaim the gospel to you also who are in Rome. 16 For I am not ashamed of the gospel; it is the power of God for salvation to everyone who has faith, to the Jew first and also to the Greek. 17 For in it the righteousness of God is revealed through faith for faith; as it is written, 'The one who is righteous will live by faith.'

Paul introduces himself, summarises his message, mentions the purpose of his letter, identifies and greets his readers, extends a greeting, prays for his readers, outlines his plans, and gives the theme of the letter.

First, Paul quotes a version of basic belief:
the gospel concerning his Son,
who was descended from David according to the flesh
and was declared to be Son of God with power
according to the spirit of holiness
by resurrection from the dead, Jesus Christ our Lord
(1:3-4).
It is likely that Paul includes this statement of faith to assure his readers of his orthodoxy. The good news is centred on Jesus the Messiah who is descended from King David on the human level and who is declared God's Son on the level of the Holy Spirit by a powerful act that raised him from the dead.

Second, Paul greets his readers in a special way:
Grace to you and peace from God our Father and the Lord Jesus Christ (1:7b).
As the Bauer Lexicon says, 'A new and characteristic development is the combination of the Greek epistolary greeting *chairein* with a Hebrew expression in the Pauline and post-Pauline letters *charis kai eirene*.' The Greek word for peace is *eirene* and translates the traditional Jewish greeting *shalom*. Paul utilises two words which resonate for both Jew and Greek. That is to say, Paul writes to both Jew and Greek with his universal message of the divine favour and messianic peace of God in Christ.

Third, Paul spells out the letter's theme:
For I am not ashamed of the gospel; it is the power of God for salvation to everyone who has faith, to the Jew first and also to the Greek. For in it the righteousness of God is revealed through faith for faith; as it is written, 'The one who is righteous will live by faith.' (1:16-17)

Paul equates the good news with God's power for salvation and the divine righteousness through faith. He is using significant terms: *power, salvation, faith, Jew, Greek, righteousness*. Indeed, *power* is parallel to *righteousness*. They combine to tell of God's way of righting wrong and speak of believers who are put right and gain life through faith in accordance with the words of Habakkuk 2:4.

Fred Craddock was a gifted preacher and biblical scholar. He recalled the occasion when a young Emory University student visited him in his office. She was not a churchgoer. She had intended to take her life by jumping off a high bridge. She stopped when a Bible verse came into her mind: 'My life is not my own. I have been bought with a price.' She asked Dr Craddock to explain what had happened to her. He engaged in conversation with her about reading the Bible and going to church. She was not reading the Bible and she did not go to church. All she could remember was her grandmother taking her as a little girl to Vacation Bible School where she wrote sentences on slips of paper and memorised them. The young woman guessed that the sentences must have been Bible verses. Dr Craddock suggested that God had stored the word of the gospel in her heart for such a time as this.

Prayer

Lord God, by the good news of Jesus your Son you have called us to be your people and given us grace and peace. Help us to experience your saving power and to be participants in your righting wrong worldwide. We pray that people near and far may come to trust and obey you through Jesus Christ in the power of the Holy Spirit. Amen.

Discuss

1   What do we consider to be basic beliefs of a follower of Jesus today?
2   Who can we remember as experiencing God's saving power in history?
3   On the basis of Romans 1:16-17, define the gospel.

Aurelius Augustine's Story

A 32-year-old professor at the University of Milan in AD 386 had lived a life of pleasure but he was not happy. One day he was sitting in the garden of his home. He heard a child's voice calling out in Latin, 'Tolle, lege! Tolle, lege!' (Take up and read! Take up and read!) He picked up a copy of Paul's letters and read these words: *Let us live honourably as in the day, not in revelling and drunkenness, not in debauchery and licentiousness, not in quarrelling and jealousy.* He had experienced all of these things. He continued reading: *Instead, put on the Lord Jesus Christ, and make no provision for the flesh, to gratify its desires. (Romans 13:13-14)* After reading this passage, Aurelius Augustine said, 'No further would I read, nor had I any need; instantly, at the end of this sentence, a clear light flooded my heart and all the darkness of doubt vanished away'.

Augustine went on to be baptised six months later in Milan. In time he was ordained as a priest in Hippo in North Africa. Five years after his ordination he became bishop of Hippo. He opposed the heretical Manichees, the schismatic Donatists, and the deviationist Pelagians. At the same time he defended Christianity against Roman paganism. Augustine argued that the downfall of the Roman Empire was due to its own sins and idolatry, not the new faith of Christianity. Having laid the foundations of Christian theology for a thousand years, he died in his 77th year. His influence was evident in the church of the medieval period and in the thinking of the renaissance scholars and the reformation leaders of the sixteenth century.

First Major Section of the Letter

Tragedy: How is Paul's letter to the Romans sad news to Gentiles and Jews?

Romans 1:18-32 speaks of the tragedy of sin in the Gentile world.

18 For the wrath of God is revealed from heaven against all ungodliness and wickedness of those who by their wickedness suppress the truth. 19 For what can be known about God is plain to them, because God has shown it to them. 20 Ever since the creation of the world his eternal power and divine nature, invisible though they are, have been understood and seen through the things he has made. So they are without excuse; 21 for though they knew God, they did not honour him as God or give thanks to him, but they became futile in their thinking, and their senseless minds were darkened. 22 Claiming to be wise, they became fools; 23 and they exchanged the glory of the immortal God for images resembling a mortal human being or birds or four-footed animals or reptiles. 24 Therefore God gave them up in the lusts of their hearts to impurity, to the degrading of their bodies among themselves, 25 because they exchanged the truth about God for a lie and worshipped and served the creature rather than the Creator, who is blessed for ever! Amen. 26 For this reason God gave them up to degrading passions. Their women exchanged natural intercourse for unnatural, 27 and in the same way also the men, giving up natural intercourse with women, were consumed with passion for one another. Men committed shameless acts with men and received in their own persons the due penalty for their error. 28 And since they did not see fit to acknowledge God, God gave them up to a debased mind and to things that should not be done. 29 They were filled with every kind of wickedness, evil, covetousness, malice. Full of envy, murder, strife, deceit, craftiness, they are gossips, 30 slanderers, God-haters, insolent, haughty, boastful, inventors of evil, rebellious towards parents, 31 foolish, faithless, heartless, ruthless. 32 They know God's decree, that those who practise such things deserve to die—yet they not only do them but even applaud others who practise them.

The revelation of God's wrath in verse 18 is parallel to the revelation of his righteousness in verse 17. God's wrath expresses his righteousness. *For the wrath of God is revealed from heaven against all ungodliness and wickedness of those who by their wickedness suppress the truth (1:18).*

Understanding Paul's concept of God's wrath is a difficult task for modern readers. God's wrath is **not** the vindictive emotion of an angry deity. It has been interpreted to mean 'an inevitable process of cause and effect in a moral universe.' However, there seems to more than an impersonal process at work in the revelation of both God's righteousness and God's wrath. Wrath is God's personal but neither a malicious nor an emotional reaction to sin. God expresses his love and mercy to all in Christ as well as his indignation against all the sin of humanity. God's wrath is opposed to *ungodliness and wickedness.* Although Gentiles have the testimony of God's *eternal power and divine nature (1:20)* in the natural order, God is not honoured and thanked. They indulge in futile thought. The wisdom of God is replaced by human foolishness in three ways.

First is the sin of idolatry: *they exchanged the glory of the immortal God for images ... Therefore God gave them up in the lusts of their hearts to impurity (1:23-24).* The Old Testament history is littered with examples of the idols of Mesopotamia, Egypt, Assyria, Babylon, Persia, and Greece. The people of Israel also were tempted by the golden calf of the exodus, the fertility gods of the promised land, the false objects of worship in the northern and southern kingdoms. In New Testament times, the gods of Rome, including the Caesars, contrasted with the worship of the God and Father of the Lord Jesus Christ.

Second is the sin of dysfunctional sexuality: *they exchanged the truth about God for a lie and worshipped and served the creature rather than the Creator ... For this reason God gave them up to degrading passions (1:25-26).* The sexual ethics of Jews and Christians in the first century contrast markedly with the permissive practices of the Greco Roman world. Paul argues that homosexual practices are a sign that society is guilty of idolatry with the result that the divine order is broken in pieces.

Lest we become preoccupied with same-sex relationships, it is worth broadening our focus to consider both homosexual and heterosexual practice. In the *Smyth & Helwys Bible Commentary* Talbert outlines four attitudes toward sex in society. 'The first holds that sex is vile. So flee it; abstain. The second maintains that sex is necessary, yet debasing. So be embarrassed about it when you, of necessity, engage in it. The third contends that sex is the be-all and end-all of life. So revel in it with no restraints. Push the boundaries! The fourth believes sex is God's good gift to be used joyously and responsibly as the Creator intended: within heterosexual marriage. So enjoy it God's way.'

Third is the sin of debased thought and anti-social vice: *since they did not see fit to acknowledge God, God gave them up to a debased mind and to things that should not be done (1:28).* In the following verses there are crimes against community (*wickedness, evil, covetousness, malice*) and crimes against persons (*envy, murder, strife, deceit, craftiness*). There are attitudes of pride (*gossips, slanderers, God-haters, insolent, haughty, boastful*) and attitudes of negativity (*inventors of evil, rebellious toward parents, foolish, faithless, heartless, ruthless*).

In *Not Ashamed of the Gospel* Rutledge recalls the 1973 publication of a book called *Whatever Became of Sin?* by the noted psychiatrist Karl Menninger. In a chapter entitled 'The Disappearance of Sin: An Eyewitness Account' Menninger says that we have crime, neurosis, symptoms, errors in judgement, self-destructive behaviour, and anti-social tendencies but we do not have sin! Menninger's exact words are memorable: 'Sin traditionally implies guilt, answerability, and ... responsibility in all human acts ... My proposal is for the revival or reassertion of personal responsibility in all human acts.'

Prayer

Lord God, although we have the testimony of your eternal power and divine nature in the natural order, there are times when we do not honour and thank you. Help us to beware of replacing your wise ways with our foolish indulgence. Give us wisdom to avoid the sins of idolatry, dysfunctional sexuality, debased thought and anti-social vice. We pray in the name of Jesus your Son and our Saviour. Amen.

Discuss

1 Three times in Romans 1, to what did God 'give them up'?
2 How do we discern right from wrong in our post Christian society?
3 Which sins are most condemned and which sins are most neglected in our world?

All You Need is Good News

Romans 2:1-3:8 speaks of the tragedy of sin in the Jewish world.

1 Therefore you have no excuse, whoever you are, when you judge others; for in passing judgement on another you condemn yourself, because you, the judge, are doing the very same things. 2 You say, 'We know that God's judgement on those who do such things is in accordance with truth.' 3 Do you imagine, whoever you are, that when you judge those who do such things and yet do them yourself, you will escape the judgement of God? 4 Or do you despise the riches of his kindness and forbearance and patience? Do you not realize that God's kindness is meant to lead you to repentance? 5 But by your hard and impenitent heart you are storing up wrath for yourself on the day of wrath, when God's righteous judgement will be revealed. 6 For he will repay according to each one's deeds: 7 to those who by patiently doing good seek for glory and honour and immortality, he will give eternal life; 8 while for those who are self-seeking and who obey not the truth but wickedness, there will be wrath and fury. 9 There will be anguish and distress for everyone who does evil, the Jew first and also the Greek, 10 but glory and honour and peace for everyone who does good, the Jew first and also the Greek. 11 For God shows no partiality. 12 All who have sinned apart from the law will also perish apart from the law, and all who have sinned under the law will be judged by the law. 13 For it is not the hearers of the law who are righteous in God's sight, but the doers of the law who will be justified. 14 When Gentiles, who do not possess the law, do instinctively what the law requires, these, though not having the law, are a law to themselves. 15 They show that what the law requires is written on their hearts, to which their own conscience also bears witness; and their conflicting thoughts will accuse or perhaps excuse them 16 on the day when, according to my gospel, God, through Jesus Christ, will judge the secret thoughts of all. 17 But if you call yourself a Jew and rely on the law and boast of your relation to God 18 and know his will and determine what is best because you are instructed in the law, 19 and if you are sure that you are a guide to the blind, a light to those who are in darkness, 20 a corrector of the foolish, a teacher of children, having in the law the embodiment of knowledge and truth, 21 you, then, that teach others, will you not teach yourself? While you preach against stealing, do you steal? 22 You that forbid adultery, do you commit adultery? You that abhor idols, do you rob temples? 23 You that boast in the law, do you dishonour God by breaking the law? 24 For, as it is written, 'The name of God is blasphemed among the Gentiles because of you.' 25 Circumcision indeed is of value if you obey the law; but if you break the law, your circumcision has become uncircumcision. 26 So, if those who are uncircumcised keep the requirements of the law, will not their uncircumcision be regarded as circumcision? 27 Then those who are physically uncircumcised but keep the law will condemn you that have the written code and circumcision but break the law. 28 For a person is not a Jew who is one outwardly, nor is true circumcision something external and physical. 29 Rather, a person is a Jew who is one inwardly, and real circumcision is a matter of the heart—it is spiritual and not literal. Such a person receives praise not from others but from God. 1 Then what advantage has the Jew? Or what is the value of circumcision? 2 Much, in every way. For in the first place the Jews were entrusted with the oracles of God. 3 What if some were unfaithful? Will their faithlessness nullify the faithfulness of God? 4 By no means! Although everyone is a liar, let God be proved true, as it is written, 'So that you may be justified in your words, and prevail in your judging.' 5 But if our injustice serves to confirm the justice of God, what should we say? That God is unjust to inflict wrath on us? (I speak in a human way.) 6 By no means! For then how could God judge the world? 7 But if through my falsehood God's truthfulness abounds to his glory, why am I still being condemned as a sinner? 8 And why not say (as some people slander us by saying that we say), 'Let us do evil so that good may come'? Their condemnation is deserved!

In this section Paul engages in an imaginary argument with a fellow Jew. After his indictment of the Gentile world in Romans 1:18-32, Paul reminds his readers: *There will be anguish and distress for everyone who does evil, the Jew first and also the Greek, but glory and honour and peace for everyone who does good, the Jew first and also the Greek. For God shows no partiality. All who have sinned apart from the law will also perish apart from the law, and all who have sinned under the law will be judged by the law (2:9-12).*

So it's important for the Jew not to judge the Gentile. One thinks of the words of Jesus: *Why do you see the speck in your neighbour's eye, but do not notice the log in your own eye? Or how can you say to your neighbour, "Let me take the speck out of your eye", while the log is in your own eye? You hypocrite, first take the log out of your own eye, and then you will see clearly to take the speck out of your neighbour's eye (Matthew 7:3-5).*

According to Paul, his fellow Jew is being a hypocrite, displaying a false sense of superiority, and failing to fulfil his destiny.

First, there is blatant hypocrisy: *In passing judgement on another you condemn yourself, because you, the judge, are doing the very same things ... While you preach against stealing, do you steal? You that forbid adultery, do you commit adultery? You that abhor idols, do you rob temples? (2:1, 21-22)*

Second, there is a false sense of superiority: *If you call yourself a Jew and rely on the law and boast of your relation to God and know his will and determine what is best because you are instructed in the law ... you, then, that teach others, will you not teach yourself? (2:18, 21)*

Third, there is a failure to fulfil his destiny: You are meant to be *a guide to the blind, a light to those who are in darkness, a corrector of the foolish, a teacher of children* and *the Jews were entrusted with the oracles of God (2:19-20; 3:2).*

In the midst of his argument Paul speaks of circumcision. the external mark of a male Jew. On the one hand, *Circumcision indeed is of value if you obey the law; but if you break the law, your circumcision has become uncircumcision. So, if those who are uncircumcised keep the requirements of the law, will not their uncircumcision be regarded as circumcision?(2:25-26)* On the other hand, *For a person is not a Jew who is one outwardly, nor is true circumcision something external and physical. Rather, a person is a Jew who is one inwardly, and real circumcision is a matter of the heart—it is spiritual and not literal (2:28-29).*

It is very important to stress that the argument of Paul is with an imaginary Jew. There were law-abiding Jews and non-observant Jews in Paul's day. Indeed, there was a spectrum of Jewish life including Sadducees, Pharisees, Essenes, Zealots, and commoners. We would be gravely mistaken to use this section to indulge in anti-Semitism. Paul himself acknowledges his Jewish heritage later in his letter: *My kindred according to the flesh ... are Israelites, and to them belong the adoption, the glory, the covenants, the giving of the law, the worship, and the promises; to them belong the patriarchs, and from them, according to the flesh, comes the Messiah, who is over all, God blessed for ever. Amen (9:3-5).*

Prayer

Lord God, we are followers of Jesus the Jewish Messiah. We give thanks for your gifts through the Jews, your ancient people. As we read Paul's imaginary argument with a fellow Jew, teach us to avoid blatant hypocrisy, to resist a false sense of superiority, and to succeed in fulfilling our destiny as light in darkness. Whether we are Jew or Gentile let us learn that the real member of God's people is one inwardly and the rite of belonging is a matter of the heart. We pray in the name of Jesus the Jewish Messiah and the Gentile King. Amen.

Discuss

1. How can we avoid blatant hypocrisy or false superiority?
2. What is the value of religious rituals, e.g. circumcision for Jews and baptism for Christians?
3. Who has greater responsibility to God: one who knows or one who does not know the Bible's teaching? Why?

All You Need is Good News

*Old City
Jerusalem*

All You Need is Good News

Romans 3:9-20 speaks of the tragedy of sin in all the world, Jew and Gentile.

9 What then? Are we any better off? No, not at all; for we have already charged that all, both Jews and Greeks, are under the power of sin, 10 as it is written: 'There is no one who is righteous, not even one; 11 there is no one who has understanding, there is no one who seeks God. 12 All have turned aside, together they have become worthless; there is no one who shows kindness, there is not even one.' 13 'Their throats are opened graves; they use their tongues to deceive.' 'The venom of vipers is under their lips.' 14 'Their mouths are full of cursing and bitterness.' 15 'Their feet are swift to shed blood; 16 ruin and misery are in their paths, 17 and the way of peace they have not known.' 18 'There is no fear of God before their eyes.' 19 Now we know that whatever the law says, it speaks to those who are under the law, so that every mouth may be silenced, and the whole world may be held accountable to God. 20 For 'no human being will be justified in his sight' by deeds prescribed by the law, for through the law comes the knowledge of sin.

Paul has portrayed Gentiles as rebellious (1:18-32) and Jews as unfaithful (2:1-3:8). Now he portrays all people under the power of sin (3:9-20).

In a string of quotations from the Hebrew Bible, Paul charges that all people are under the power of sin.

First, sin affects our relationship with God: *'There is no one who is righteous, not even one; there is no one who has understanding, there is no one who seeks God. All have turned aside, together they have become worthless; there is no one who shows kindness, there is not even one.' (3:10b-12)*

Second, sin damages our sense of self-esteem: *'Their throats are opened graves; they use their tongues to deceive.' 'The venom of vipers is under their lips.' 'Their mouths are full of cursing and bitterness.' (3:13-14)*

Third, sin corrupts our human relationships: *'Their feet are swift to shed blood; ruin and misery are in their paths, and the way of peace they have not known.' 'There is no fear of God before their eyes.' (3:15-18)*

He concludes with the notion of the accountability of every human being before the God of the whole world: *Now we know that whatever the law says, it speaks to those who are under the law, so that every mouth may be silenced, and the whole world may be held accountable to God. For 'no human being will be justified in his sight' by deeds prescribed by the law, for through the law comes the knowledge of sin (3:19-20).* Apart from faith, all people experience the absence of God and the presence of sin in a dark and empty world.

There is a plaque behind the pulpit of a church on the island of Aneityum, Vanuatu, in honour of John Geddie: 'In memory of John Geddie, D.D., born in Scotland, 1815, minister in Prince Edward Island seven years, Missionary sent from Nova Scotia to Aneityum for twenty-four years. When he landed in 1848, there were no Christians here, and when he left in 1872 there were no heathen.'

Prayer

Most merciful God, Father of our Lord Jesus Christ, we confess that we have sinned in thought, word and deed. We have not loved you with our whole heart. We have not loved our neighbours as ourselves. In your mercy forgive what we have been, help us to amend what we are, and direct what we shall be; that we may do justly, love mercy, and walk humbly with you, our God. In the name of Jesus we pray. Amen.

Discuss

1   What are some effects of sin?
2   What are some ways forward out of our sinfulness?
3   How and why does Paul value the Old Testament?

Martin Luther's Story

A 34-year-old professor at the University of Wittenberg in 1517 had lived a life of austerity but he was not happy. As part of his teaching duties, he studied and lectured on Paul's letters to the Galatians and the Romans. He was puzzled by the references to the righteousness and wrath of God. Finally, Martin Luther came to the realisation that the righteousness of God is not something that people achieve but it is something that people receive. He also discovered that the wrath of God is not something that a spiteful God dispenses but it is something that a loving Saviour suffers in the place of the penitent sinner. This was the beginning of Luther's rediscovery of the Pauline teaching of justification by faith.

Luther challenged the theology and practice of the Roman Catholic Church. He started by publishing his *95 Theses* which arose out of his objection to the selling of indulgences, documents sold by the church and bought by individuals to secure the forgiveness of sins for themselves or on behalf of the dead. Luther's challenge then asserted the authority of the Scriptures to be superior to the authority of the Pope. He argued that all Christians were priests, that there were not seven but two sacraments, and that Christians were free from church laws but not from the law of love. By the time that Luther died in 1546, he had caused the church to be reformed in theology and practice. Priests married, the Bible was in the language of the people, hymns were written, and a catechism was produced. The influence of Luther spread to the other leaders and the main movements of the sixteenth century Protestant Reformation.

All You Need is Good News

*River Tiber
Rome*

Second Major Section of the Letter

Comedy: How is Paul's letter to the Romans glad news to all who believe?

Romans 3:21-31 talks about the comedy, the glad news in Jesus Christ: judge, benefactor, priest.

21 But now, irrespective of law, the righteousness of God has been disclosed, and is attested by the law and the prophets, 22 the righteousness of God through faith in Jesus Christ for all who believe. For there is no distinction, 23 since all have sinned and fall short of the glory of God; 24 they are now justified by his grace as a gift, through the redemption that is in Christ Jesus, 25 whom God put forward as a sacrifice of atonement by his blood, effective through faith. He did this to show his righteousness, because in his divine forbearance he had passed over the sins previously committed; 26 it was to prove at the present time that he himself is righteous and that he justifies the one who has faith in Jesus. 27 Then what becomes of boasting? It is excluded. By what law? By that of works? No, but by the law of faith. 28 For we hold that a person is justified by faith apart from works prescribed by the law. 29 Or is God the God of Jews only? Is he not the God of Gentiles also? Yes, of Gentiles also, 30 since God is one; and he will justify the circumcised on the ground of faith and the uncircumcised through that same faith. 31 Do we then overthrow the law by this faith? By no means! On the contrary, we uphold the law.

We may summarise this section as follows. Apart from law, God has revealed his way of righting wrong. It is in accord with the Mosaic Law and the Old Testament Prophets. It is available to all who put their faith in Jesus. All are sinners but may be justified, redeemed, and atoned for. In the past God showed his patience. In the present God offers his pardon. Boasting is not excluded by the law of works and trusting in God of Jew and Gentile is included by the law of faith. In other words, The glad news is that God extends his saving power through Christ's death.

What is the meaning of law? There are four interpretations for the phrase *works of the law (3:20)*: the ceremonial law; the social boundary markers (circumcision, food laws, Sabbath); the legalistic keeping of the law; the 613 commandments of the law.

What does God's righteousness mean? *But now, apart from law, the righteousness of God has been disclosed ... the righteousness of God through faith in Jesus Christ (3:21-22).* As we noted in relation to 1:16-17, Paul equates the good news with God's power for salvation and the divine righteousness through faith. God's *power* is parallel to God's *righteousness*. They tell of God's way of righting wrong and speak of believers who are put right and gain life through faith.

What is sin? *For there is no distinction ... all have sinned and fall short of the glory of God (3:22-23).* According to the Bauer Lexicon to *have sinned* means 'miss the mark, err, do wrong' and to *fall short* means 'be lacking, go without.' Paul is probably referring *both* to the glory lost in humankind's fall *and* to the glory that fallen humankind is failing to reach as a result.

What are the meanings of 'justified, redeemed, and atoned for'? *They are now justified by his grace as a gift, through the redemption that is in Christ Jesus, whom God put forward as a sacrifice of atonement ... (3:24-25)* Paul uses three metaphors to describe the work of Christ inaugurating the new age: the law court, the institution of slavery, the ritual of sacrifice. In the *Moffatt New Testament Commentary* Dodd's analysis is helpful. 'In the first, God takes the part of the judge who acquits the prisoner; in the second, that of the benefactor who secures freedom for the slave; in the third, that of the priest who makes expiation.' Each metaphor has associations. Justification reminds the reader of the last judgement: *we will all stand before the judgement seat of God ... each of us will be accountable to God (Romans 14:10, 12).* Redemption recalls the liberation of the Israelites from Egypt: *the Lord has brought you out with a mighty hand, and redeemed you from the house of slavery, from the hand of Pharaoh king of Egypt (Deuteronomy 7:8).* Atonement is associated with *the mercy-seat* of the tabernacle in Exodus 25 and Leviticus 16.

The meaning of the Greek word *hilastērion* has been debated. Dodd interpreted it as expiation, a means by which guilt is annulled. He argued that propitiation was a misleading translation, suggesting the placating of an angry God in terms of pagan usage but not in accord with biblical usage. Indeed, the Bauer Lexicon notes: 'The unique feature relative to Greco-Roman usage is the initiative taken by God to effect removal of impediments to a relationship with God's self.' However, Morris asserted that propitiation meant the removal of wrath and was unacceptable to some scholars with an aversion to the concept of wrath. Perhaps the resolution of the matter is as the Bauer Lexicon indicates: 'The Septuagint uses *hilastērion* of the lid on the ark of the covenant, *kipporeth*, which was sprinkled with the blood of the sin-offering on the Day of Atonement.' The differing understandings are seen in the NRSV: *a sacrifice of atonement*; the NRSV margin: *a place of atonement*; and the REB: *the means of expiating sin.*

What is faith? *The righteousness of God* is *through faith in Jesus Christ ... (3:22)* The majority interpret *dia pisteōs Iēsou Christou* as an objective genitive as in the NRSV: *through faith in Jesus Christ.* A vocal minority interpret the phrase as a subjective genitive as in the NRSV margin: *through the faith(fulness) of Jesus Christ.*

What is the contrast between boasting and trusting? *Then what becomes of boasting? It is excluded. By what law? By that of works? No, but by the law of faith. For we hold that a person is justified by faith apart from works prescribed by the law. (3:28-29)* Paul finally contrasts boasting in the law of works and trusting in the law of faith. On the one hand, he appears to speak of the Jew who boasts in his national identity markers of circumcision, food laws, and Sabbath. On the other hand, he prefers the faith of Jew and Gentile who trust in the God of Jesus.

Prayer

Lord God, we thank you for revealing your way of righting wrong. We acknowledge that we are sinners who by faith through grace may be justified, redeemed, and atoned for by the death of Christ. We look back and see your patience. Assist us to receive your pardon. Let us not boast in our achievements but let us trust in you, God of Jew and Gentile, and let us experience the glad news that you extend your saving power through Christ's death. In the name of Jesus we pray. Amen.

Discuss

1. How does the sad news of the first part of Romans become glad news in the second part?
2. What are the most effective ways of picturing the work of Christ on the cross?
3. Why is the cross a most significant Christian symbol?

All You Need is Good News

Romans 4:1-25 talks about the comedy, the glad news in Abraham: Example of faith and father of faithful.

1 What then are we to say was gained by Abraham, our ancestor according to the flesh? 2 For if Abraham was justified by works, he has something to boast about, but not before God. 3 For what does the scripture say? 'Abraham believed God, and it was reckoned to him as righteousness.' 4 Now to one who works, wages are not reckoned as a gift but as something due. 5 But to one who without works trusts him who justifies the ungodly, such faith is reckoned as righteousness. 6 So also David speaks of the blessedness of those to whom God reckons righteousness irrespective of works:7 'Blessed are those whose iniquities are forgiven, and whose sins are covered; 8 blessed is the one against whom the Lord will not reckon sin.' 9 Is this blessedness, then, pronounced only on the circumcised, or also on the uncircumcised? We say, 'Faith was reckoned to Abraham as righteousness.' 10 How then was it reckoned to him? Was it before or after he had been circumcised? It was not after, but before he was circumcised. 11 He received the sign of circumcision as a seal of the righteousness that he had by faith while he was still uncircumcised. The purpose was to make him the ancestor of all who believe without being circumcised and who thus have righteousness reckoned to them, 12 and likewise the ancestor of the circumcised who are not only circumcised but who also follow the example of the faith that our ancestor Abraham had before he was circumcised. 13 For the promise that he would inherit the world did not come to Abraham or to his descendants through the law but through the righteousness of faith. 14 If it is the adherents of the law who are to be the heirs, faith is null and the promise is void. 15 For the law brings wrath; but where there is no law, neither is there violation.16 For this reason it depends on faith, in order that the promise may rest on grace and be guaranteed to all his descendants, not only to the adherents of the law but also to those who share the faith of Abraham (for he is the father of all of us, 17 as it is written, 'I have made you the father of many nations')—in the presence of the God in whom he believed, who gives life to the dead and calls into existence the things that do not exist. 18 Hoping against hope, he believed that he would become 'the father of many nations', according to what was said, 'So numerous shall your descendants be.' 19 He did not weaken in faith when he considered his own body, which was already as good as dead (for he was about a hundred years old), or when he considered the barrenness of Sarah's womb. 20 No distrust made him waver concerning the promise of God, but he grew strong in his faith as he gave glory to God, 21 being fully convinced that God was able to do what he had promised. 22 Therefore his faith 'was reckoned to him as righteousness.'

23 Now the words, 'it was reckoned to him', were written not for his sake alone, 24 but for ours also. It will be reckoned to us who believe in him who raised Jesus our Lord from the dead, 25 who was handed over to death for our trespasses and was raised for our justification.

In this chapter Father Abraham is an abiding example of faith. And more than that, Abraham is Father of the faithful.

Paul's readers would have regarded Abraham as their ancestor *according to the flesh (4:1)*, that is, by natural descent. As Joshua had said, *'Thus says the LORD, the God of Israel: Long ago your ancestors ... lived beyond the Euphrates and served other gods. Then I took your father Abraham from beyond the River and led him through all the land of Canaan and made his offspring many.'(Joshua 24:2-3)* Paul argues that Abraham was not justified, that is, put right with God by anything he did. Rather, *'Abraham believed God, and it was reckoned to him as righteousness.'(4:3 quoting Genesis 15:6)*

Paul reinforces his argument by citing David, the traditional author of the Psalms, who said, *'Blessed are those whose iniquities are forgiven, and whose sins are covered; blessed is the one against whom the Lord will not reckon sin.'(4:7-8 quoting Psalm 32:1-2)*

If *'Faith was reckoned to Abraham as righteousness'(4:9)*, when was Abraham put right with God? *Was it before or after he had been circumcised?(4:10)* In fact, Paul contrasts Genesis 15:6, when Abraham was justified by faith, with Genesis 17:9-14, when Abraham was circumcised in the flesh. Therefore, Abraham is *the ancestor of all who believe without being circumcised and who thus have righteousness reckoned to them, and likewise the ancestor of the circumcised ... who also follow the example of the faith that our ancestor Abraham had ... (4:11-12)*

God's dealings with Abraham are characterised by *the promise that he would inherit the world (4:13). This promise is given to all his descendants, not only to the adherents of the law but also to those who share the faith of Abraham ... he is the father of all of us, as it is written, 'I have made you the father of many nations'(4:16-17 quoting Genesis 17:5)*. Abraham had faith in God *who gives life to the dead and calls into existence the things that do not exist (4:17)*.

Although Abraham and Sarah were past the age of child bearing, *No distrust made him waver concerning the promise of God, but he grew strong in his faith as he gave glory to God, being fully convinced that God was able to do what he had promised. Therefore his faith 'was reckoned to him as righteousness.' (4:20-22)*

The logic of grace does not apply to Abraham alone. *Now the words, 'it was reckoned to him', were written not for his sake alone, but for ours also. It will be reckoned to us who believe in him who raised Jesus our Lord from the dead, who was handed over to death for our trespasses and was raised for our justification (4:23-25)*.

The kind of God in whom Abraham and the early Christians trusted is the one *who gives life to the dead* and *who raised Jesus our Lord from the dead (4:17, 24)*. Both Abraham and those who trust in Christ share faith in God who can bring life out of death. Verse 25 probably ends with an early Christian confession of faith: Christ died that our sins might be forgiven; Christ was raised that we might be put right with God.

Chapter 4 undoubtedly speaks of faith in God's raising Jesus from the dead. Although there may be unending discussion about the form that Jesus' resurrection took and about the proclamation of Jesus' resurrection from then to now, for Paul it seems that it is impossible to be a Christian who does not in some sense believe in Jesus' resurrection.

Prayer

Lord God, we thank you for the inspirational example of Father Abraham's faith. Help us trust in you, God of all, Jew and Gentile, and let us experience your grace and peace in tough times. We thank you that Abraham is Father of the faithful and that the logic of grace does not apply to Abraham alone. Assist us to share the resurrection faith that you can bring life out of death and despair. In the name of Jesus we pray. Amen.

Discuss

1 What do we remember of Abraham's story in Genesis?
2 How does Abraham's faith make an impact in ancient and modern times?
3 Is it possible to be a Christian who does not in some sense believe in Jesus' resurrection?

Romans 5:1-21 talks about the comedy, the glad news in grace instead of wrath.

1 Therefore, since we are justified by faith, we have peace with God through our Lord Jesus Christ, 2 through whom we have obtained access to this grace in which we stand; and we boast in our hope of sharing the glory of God. 3 And not only that, but we also boast in our sufferings, knowing that suffering produces endurance, 4 and endurance produces character, and character produces hope, 5 and hope does not disappoint us, because God's love has been poured into our hearts through the Holy Spirit that has been given to us. 6 For while we were still weak, at the right time Christ died for the ungodly. 7 Indeed, rarely will anyone die for a righteous person— though perhaps for a good person someone might actually dare to die. 8 But God proves his love for us in that while we still were sinners Christ died for us. 9 Much more surely then, now that we have been justified by his blood, will we be saved through him from the wrath of God. 10 For if while we were enemies, we were reconciled to God through the death of his Son, much more surely, having been reconciled, will we be saved by his life. 11 But more than that, we even boast in God through our Lord Jesus Christ, through whom we have now received reconciliation. 12 Therefore, just as sin came into the world through one man, and death came through sin, and so death spread to all because all have sinned— 13 sin was indeed in the world before the law, but sin is not reckoned when there is no law. 14 Yet death exercised dominion from Adam to Moses, even over those whose sins were not like the transgression of Adam, who is a type of the one who was to come. 15 But the free gift is not like the trespass. For if the many died through the one man's trespass, much more surely have the grace of God and the free gift in the grace of the one man, Jesus Christ, abounded for the many. 16 And the free gift is not like the effect of the one man's sin. For the judgement following one trespass brought condemnation, but the free gift following many trespasses brings justification. 17 If, because of the one man's trespass, death exercised dominion through that one, much more surely will those who receive the abundance of grace and the free gift of righteousness exercise dominion in life through the one man, Jesus Christ. 18 Therefore just as one man's trespass led to condemnation for all, so one man's act of righteousness leads to justification and life for all. 19 For just as by the one man's disobedience the many were made sinners, so by the one man's obedience the many will be made righteous. 20 But law came in, with the result that the trespass multiplied; but where sin increased, grace abounded all the more, 21 so that, just as sin exercised dominion in death, so grace might also exercise dominion through justification leading to eternal life through Jesus Christ our Lord.

In *Beyond Words* Buechner says, 'The grace of God means something like: "Here is your life. You might never have been, but you are, because the party wouldn't have been complete without you. Here is the world. Beautiful and terrible things will happen. Don't be afraid. I am with you. Nothing can ever separate us. It's for you I created the universe. I love you." There's only one catch. Like any other gift, the gift of grace can be yours only if you'll reach out and take it.'

Paul uses memorable words to assure his readers that they have been justified by faith. As we saw in 3:24-25, one of his compelling metaphors is the law court: God is the judge who acquits the prisoner. Here Paul spells out three results of being put right with God by faith. *Therefore, since we are justified by faith, we have **peace** with God through our Lord Jesus Christ, through whom we have obtained access to this **grace** in which we stand; and we boast in our **hope** of sharing the glory of God (5:1-2).*

Accordingly, the believer can boast in suffering because *suffering produces endurance, and endurance produces character, and character produces hope (5:3-4).* Most of all, there is the basis of the believer's hope: *hope does not disappoint us, because God's love has been poured into our hearts through the Holy Spirit that has been given to us (5:5).* Paul himself knows that hope is the joyful expectation of future good which is based on the past experience of God's faithfulness.

Furthermore, Paul says, *God proves his love for us in that while we still were sinners Christ died for us (5:8).* All of this relates to people who are *weak ... ungodly ... sinners ... enemies (5:6,*

8, 10). As God brings out the fact of his love, simultaneously he brings it home to us. God's saving power includes past, present, and future. Believers *have been justified by his blood ... will be saved through him from the wrath ... were reconciled to God through the death of his Son ... will be saved by his life ... through our Lord Jesus Christ ... have received reconciliation (5:9-11)*.

The second half of the chapter contrasts two realms of existence represented by Adam and Christ. On the one hand, in Adam law, sin, and death are at work. On the other hand, in Christ grace, righteousness, and life are in operation. In the *Word Biblical Commentary* Dunn comments thoughtfully: 'Indeed ... we should say that the effect of the comparison between the two epochal figures, Adam and Christ, is not so much to historicize the individual Adam as to bring out the more than individual significance of the historic Christ.'

Paul's understanding of Adam is based on Genesis 2-3. *Therefore, just as sin came into the world through one man, and death came through sin, and so death spread to all because all have sinned (5:12)*. Then he understands Moses' role as lawgiver to be the reckoning of sin: *sin was indeed in the world before the law, but sin is not reckoned when there is no law (5:13)*. He spells out the contrast between Adam and Christ: *For if the many died through the one man's trespass, much more surely have the grace of God and the free gift in the grace of the one man, Jesus Christ, abounded for the many ... For the judgement following one trespass brought condemnation, but the free gift following many trespasses brings justification (5:15-16)*.

Finally he explains the connections between sin, law, and death: *But law came in, with the result that the trespass multiplied; but where sin increased, grace abounded all the more, so that, just as sin exercised dominion in death, so grace might also exercise dominion through justification leading to eternal life through Jesus Christ our Lord (5:20-21).* In so doing, after dealing with freedom from wrath in chapter 5, Paul is looking forward to freedom from sin in chapter 6, freedom from law in chapter 7, and freedom from death in chapter 8.

Prayer

Lord God, we thank you for the glad news of freedom from your indignation against all the sin of humanity and freedom towards your expression of love and mercy to all in Christ. Help us to trust in the midst of suffering and to have hope in your love which has been poured into our hearts through the Holy Spirit, and to find the proof of your love in that while we still were sinners Christ died for us. Bring us from law to grace, from sin to righteousness, and from death to life. In the name of Jesus we pray. Amen.

Discuss

1   What are ways in which we experience hope and find assurance despite trials and tests in life?
2   How does God's saving power include past, present, and future?
3   Does it matter if we think of Adam as fictional and Christ as factual?

All You Need is Good News

Romans 6:1-23 talks about the comedy, the glad news in eternal life instead of sin.

1 What then are we to say? Should we continue in sin in order that grace may abound? 2 By no means! How can we who died to sin go on living in it? 3 Do you not know that all of us who have been baptized into Christ Jesus were baptized into his death? 4 Therefore we have been buried with him by baptism into death, so that, just as Christ was raised from the dead by the glory of the Father, so we too might walk in newness of life. 5 For if we have been united with him in a death like his, we will certainly be united with him in a resurrection like his. 6 We know that our old self was crucified with him so that the body of sin might be destroyed, and we might no longer be enslaved to sin. 7 For whoever has died is freed from sin. 8 But if we have died with Christ, we believe that we will also live with him. 9 We know that Christ, being raised from the dead, will never die again; death no longer has dominion over him. 10 The death he died, he died to sin, once for all; but the life he lives, he lives to God. 11 So you also must consider yourselves dead to sin and alive to God in Christ Jesus. 12 Therefore, do not let sin exercise dominion in your mortal bodies, to make you obey their passions. 13 No longer present your members to sin as instruments of wickedness, but present yourselves to God as those who have been brought from death to life, and present your members to God as instruments of righteousness. 14 For sin will have no dominion over you, since you are not under law but under grace. 15 What then? Should we sin because we are not under law but under grace? By no means! 16 Do you not know that if you present yourselves to anyone as obedient slaves, you are slaves of the one whom you obey, either of sin, which leads to death, or of obedience, which leads to righteousness? 17 But thanks be to God that you, having once been slaves of sin, have become obedient from the heart to the form of teaching to which you were entrusted, 18 and that you, having been set free from sin, have become slaves of righteousness. 19 I am speaking in human terms because of your natural limitations. For just as you once presented your members as slaves to impurity and to greater and greater iniquity, so now present your members as slaves to righteousness for sanctification. 20 When you were slaves of sin, you were free in regard to righteousness. 21 So what advantage did you then get from the things of which you now are ashamed? The end of those things is death. 22 But now that you have been freed from sin and enslaved to God, the advantage you get is sanctification. The end is eternal life. 23 For the wages of sin is death, but the free gift of God is eternal life in Christ Jesus our Lord.

Chapter 6 puts paid to a dangerous half-truth that God accepts people as they are. The whole truth is God accepts people where they are, but God does not intend to leave them where they are.

First, Paul deals with dying to sin in verses 1-11. Among the objections to justification by faith are two ideas: *What then are we to say? Should we continue in sin in order that grace may abound? ... What then? Should we sin because we are not under law but under grace?(6:1,15)* In both cases Paul says: *By no means!* He answers such questions with a question: *How can we who died to sin go on living in it?(6:2)*

Indeed, the end of sin's power is seen in baptism. *Do you not know that all of us who have been baptized into Christ Jesus were baptized into his death? Therefore we have been buried with him by baptism into death, so that, just as Christ was raised from the dead by the glory of the Father, so we too might walk in newness of life (6:3-4).*

Christian baptism of the first century was immersion of believers. It had six associations: purification — believers are cleansed and forgiven (Romans 6:3); identification — believers belong to God (Acts 2:38); incorporation — believers join God's people (1 Corinthians 12:13); regeneration — believers are born anew (Titus 4:7); salvation — believers experience God's help (1 Peter 3:21); and illumination — believers find God's guidance (Hebrews 6:4).

Buechner's comment in *Beyond Words* is apt. 'Baptism consists of getting dunked or sprinkled ... Dunking is a better symbol ... Going under symbolizes the end of everything about your life that is less than human. Coming up again symbolizes the beginning in you of something strange and new and hopeful. You can breathe again.'

The body of sin is done away when *our old self was crucified with him (6:6)*. The pattern set by Christ is as follows: *The death he died, he died to sin, once for all; but the life he lives, he lives to God (6:10)*. The believers' responsibility is to *consider yourselves dead to sin and alive to God in Christ Jesus (6:11)*. The meaning of being *dead to sin and alive to God* is spelled out for believers in the second section of the chapter.

Second, Paul deals with living to God in verses 12-23. Believers are to *not let sin exercise dominion in your mortal bodies* and to *present yourselves to God as those who have been brought from death to life (6:12-13)*.

On the one hand, there is a description of what people were before they turned from darkness:

> *members to sin as instruments of wickedness (6:13)*
> *under law (6:14-15)*
> *sin ... leads to death (6:16)*
> *slaves of sin (6:17, 20)*
> *slaves to impurity and to greater and greater iniquity (6:19)*
> *end of those things is death (6:21)*
> *wages of sin is death (6:23)*

On the other hand, there is a description of what people are after they turned to light:

members to God as instruments of righteousness (6:13)
under grace (6:14-15)
obedience ... leads to righteousness (6:16)
slaves of righteousness (6:18)
slaves to righteousness for sanctification (6:19)
end is eternal life (6:22)
free gift of God is eternal life (6:23)

The contrast is drawn in terms of slavery in the first century. *Do you not know that if you present yourselves to anyone as obedient slaves, you are slaves of the one whom you obey, either of sin, which leads to death, or of obedience, which leads to righteousness?(6:16)* The two slave masters are named: *For just as you once presented your members as slaves to impurity and to greater and greater iniquity, so now present your members as slaves to righteousness for sanctification.* The outcomes of the two slaveries are apparent: *For the wages of sin is death, but the free gift of God is eternal life in Christ Jesus our Lord (6:23).* Christians are truly most free when they are servants of Christ.

Prayer

Lord God, we thank you for the glad news of eternal life instead of sin. We recall the symbolism of baptism that believers are cleansed and forgiven, belong to you, join your people, are born anew, experience your help, and find your guidance. Assist us as we turn from darkness to light. Let us die to sin and live to you. Help us to remember where we have come from, how much we've got to do, and how much we need one another to do it. In the name of Jesus we pray. Amen.

Discuss

1. What do we say if someone says that God accepts people as they are?
2. How do we assess that changes are real in the lives of ourselves and others?
3. What do we think of this statement? 'God wants to save our souls, but he is not concerned with our bodies.'

All You Need is Good News

*Temple of Apollo
Corinth*

All You Need is Good News

Romans 7:1-25 talks about the comedy, the glad news in liberation instead of law.

1 Do you not know, brothers and sisters—for I am speaking to those who know the law—that the law is binding on a person only during that person's lifetime? 2 Thus a married woman is bound by the law to her husband as long as he lives; but if her husband dies, she is discharged from the law concerning the husband. 3 Accordingly, she will be called an adulteress if she lives with another man while her husband is alive. But if her husband dies, she is free from that law, and if she marries another man, she is not an adulteress. 4 In the same way, my friends, you have died to the law through the body of Christ, so that you may belong to another, to him who has been raised from the dead in order that we may bear fruit for God. 5 While we were living in the flesh, our sinful passions, aroused by the law, were at work in our members to bear fruit for death. 6 But now we are discharged from the law, dead to that which held us captive, so that we are slaves not under the old written code but in the new life of the Spirit. 7 What then should we say? That the law is sin? By no means! Yet, if it had not been for the law, I would not have known sin. I would not have known what it is to covet if the law had not said, 'You shall not covet.' 8 But sin, seizing an opportunity in the commandment, produced in me all kinds of covetousness. Apart from the law sin lies dead. 9 I was once alive apart from the law, but when the commandment came, sin revived 10 and I died, and the very commandment that promised life proved to be death to me. 11 For sin, seizing an opportunity in the commandment, deceived me and through it killed me. 12 So the law is holy, and the commandment is holy and just and good. 13 Did what is good, then, bring death to me? By no means! It was sin, working death in me through what is good, in order that sin might be shown to be sin, and through the commandment might become sinful beyond measure. 14 For we know that the law is spiritual; but I am of the flesh, sold into slavery under sin. 15 I do not understand my own actions. For I do not do what I want, but I do the very thing I hate. 16 Now if I do what I do not want, I agree that the law is good. 17 But in fact it is no longer I that do it, but sin that dwells within me. 18 For I know that nothing good dwells within me, that is, in my flesh. I can will what is right, but I cannot do it. 19 For I do not do the good I want, but the evil I do not want is what I do. 20 Now if I do what I do not want, it is no longer I that do it, but sin that dwells within me. 21 So I find it to be a law that when I want to do what is good, evil lies close at hand. 22 For I delight in the law of God in my inmost self, 23 but I see in my members another law at war with the law of my mind, making me captive to the law of sin that dwells in my members. 24 Wretched man that I am! Who will rescue me from this body of death? 25 Thanks be to God through Jesus Christ our Lord! So then, with my mind I am a slave to the law of God, but with my flesh I am a slave to the law of sin.

The overall theme of chapter 7 is that believers have been liberated from the law which led to deadly despair.

First is an analogy of marriage and divorce: *Thus a married woman is bound by the law to her husband as long as he lives; but if her husband dies, she is discharged from the law concerning the husband ... In the same way, my friends, you have died to the law through the body of Christ, so that you may belong to another, to him who has been raised from the dead in order that we may bear fruit for God (7:2, 4).* By analogy Paul looks forward to the time when *we are discharged from the law, dead to that which held us captive, so that we are slaves not under the old written code but in the new life of the Spirit (7:6).*

Second is an argument based on the story of Adam in Genesis 2-3. The 'I' echoes the Adam of Genesis. In the process Paul distinguishes Adam before the law of Moses in verses 7-13 and humans like Adam after the law of Moses in verses 14-25. The law is not the culprit but the law is exploited by sin and death. *Yet, if it had not been for the law, I would not have known sin. I would not have known what it is to covet if the law had not said, "You shall not covet." ... For sin, seizing an opportunity in the commandment, deceived me and through it killed me. So the law is holy, and the commandment is holy and just and good (7: 7, 11-12).*

Third is the continuation of an argument which deals with humans like Adam after the law of Moses. *It was sin, working death in me through what is good, in order that sin might be shown to be sin, and through the commandment might become sinful beyond measure. For we know that the law is spiritual; but I am of the flesh, sold into slavery under sin (7:13-14).*

Sin works through the divided 'I'. *For I do not do the good I want, but the evil I do not want is what I do. Now if I do what I do not want, it is no longer I that do it, but sin that dwells within me (7:19-20).* Käsemann puts it well, '*Egō* means mankind under the shadow of Adam.'

Sin also works through the divided law. *For I delight in the law of God in my inmost self, but I see in my members another law at war with the law of my mind, making me captive to the law of sin that dwells in my members (7:22-23).* The Law should have been a guard against sin for fallen persons, but became a goad to sin, according to Paul.

Finally, Paul anticipates chapter 8: *with my mind I am a slave to the law of God (7:25a)*; and recapitulates chapter 7: *with my flesh I am a slave to the law of sin(7:25b)*.

In *Beyond Words* Buechner compares the Church with Alcoholics Anonymous. 'You can't help thinking that something like this is what the Church is meant to be and maybe once was before it got to be Big Business. Sinners Anonymous. "I can will what is right but I cannot do it," is the way Saint Paul put it, speaking for all of us. "For I do not do the good I want, but the evil I do not want is what I do" (Romans 7:19). "I am me. I am a sinner." "Hi, you." Hi, every Sadie and Sal. Hi, every Tom, Dick, and Harry. It is the forgiveness of sins, of course. It is what the Church is all about.'

We have traversed an interesting road from chapter 5 — glad news of grace instead of wrath — through chapter 6 — glad news of eternal life instead of sin — to chapter 7 — glad news of liberation instead of law — and ahead of us lies chapter 8 — glad news of the Spirit instead of death.

Prayer

Lord God, we thank you for the glad news of liberation instead of law. We think of the story of Adam who doubted the truth of the divine word and failed to obey the divine command. We identify with such doubt and disobedience in our sinfulness. We recognise the reality of our anguish when we become followers of Jesus and yet sometimes sin in thought, word, and deed. Turn our eyes upon Jesus the crucified and risen Lord who gives us his Spirit. In his name we pray. Amen.

Discuss

1   What is already and not yet in terms of God's saving power in human life?
2   How do we encourage ourselves to grow up by the grace of Christ and by knowing him?
3   What can the Church learn from Alcoholics Anonymous?

All You Need is Good News

Romans 8:1-39 talks about the comedy, the glad news in the Spirit instead of death.

Part A Romans 8:1-27 explores salvation in eight ways.

1 There is therefore now no condemnation for those who are in Christ Jesus. 2 For the law of the Spirit of life in Christ Jesus has set you free from the law of sin and of death. 3 For God has done what the law, weakened by the flesh, could not do: by sending his own Son in the likeness of sinful flesh, and to deal with sin, he condemned sin in the flesh, 4 so that the just requirement of the law might be fulfilled in us, who walk not according to the flesh but according to the Spirit. 5 For those who live according to the flesh set their minds on the things of the flesh, but those who live according to the Spirit set their minds on the things of the Spirit. 6 To set the mind on the flesh is death, but to set the mind on the Spirit is life and peace. 7 For this reason the mind that is set on the flesh is hostile to God; it does not submit to God's law—indeed it cannot, 8 and those who are in the flesh cannot please God. 9 But you are not in the flesh; you are in the Spirit, since the Spirit of God dwells in you. Anyone who does not have the Spirit of Christ does not belong to him. 10 But if Christ is in you, though the body is dead because of sin, the Spirit is life because of righteousness. 11 If the Spirit of him who raised Jesus from the dead dwells in you, he who raised Christ from the dead will give life to your mortal bodies also through his Spirit that dwells in you. 12 So then, brothers and sisters, we are debtors, not to the flesh, to live according to the flesh— 13 for if you live according to the flesh, you will die; but if by the Spirit you put to death the deeds of the body, you will live. 14 For all who are led by the Spirit of God are children of God. 15 For you did not receive a spirit of slavery to fall back into fear, but you have received a spirit of adoption. When we cry, 'Abba! Father!' 16 it is that very Spirit bearing witness with our spirit that we are children of God, 17 and if children, then heirs, heirs of God and joint heirs with Christ—if, in fact, we suffer with him so that we may also be glorified with him. 18 I consider that the sufferings of this present time are not worth comparing with the glory about to be revealed to us. 19 For the creation waits with eager longing for the revealing of the children of God; 20 for the creation was subjected to futility, not of its own will but by the will of the one who subjected it, in hope 21 that the creation itself will be set free from its bondage to decay and will obtain the freedom of the glory of the children of God. 22 We know that the whole creation has been groaning in labour pains until now; 23 and not only the creation, but we ourselves, who have the first fruits of the Spirit, groan inwardly while we wait for adoption, the redemption of our bodies. 24 For in hope we were saved. Now hope that is seen is not hope. For who hopes for what is seen? 25 But if we hope for what we do not see, we wait for it with patience. 26 Likewise the Spirit helps us in our weakness; for we do not know how to pray as we ought, but that very Spirit intercedes with sighs too deep for words. 27 And God, who searches the heart, knows what is the mind of the Spirit, because the Spirit intercedes for the saints according to the will of God.

(1) The law of the Spirit: *For the law of the Spirit of life in Christ Jesus has set you free from the law of sin and of death (8:2).* This law operates because God deals with human weakness *by sending his own Son in the likeness of sinful flesh, and as a sin offering (8:3 NRSV margin).*

(2) The mind-set of the Spirit: *For those who live according to the flesh set their minds on the things of the flesh, but those who live according to the Spirit set their minds on the things of the Spirit (8:5).* One is reminded of the Latin motto: 'Mens sana in corpore sano' which means 'A healthy mind in a healthy body'.

(3) The dwelling of the Spirit: *But you are not in the flesh; you are in the Spirit, since the Spirit of God dwells in you ... he who raised Christ from the dead will give life to your mortal bodies also through his Spirit ... (8:9, 11)* There are three stages of such indwelling: past (*not in the flesh*), present (*the Spirit of God dwells in you*), and future (*he who raised Christ from the dead will give life to your mortal bodies also through his Spirit*).

(4) The life of the Spirit: *For if you live according to the flesh, you will die; but if by the Spirit you put to death the deeds of the body, you will live (8:13).* Paul says elsewhere, *Now the works of the flesh are obvious: fornication, impurity,*

licentiousness, idolatry, sorcery, enmities, strife, jealousy, anger, quarrels, dissensions, factions, envy, drunkenness, carousing, and things like these. By contrast, the fruit of the Spirit is love, joy, peace, patience, kindness, generosity, faithfulness, gentleness, and self-control. There is no law against such things (Galatians 5:19-20, 22-23).

(5) The leading of the Spirit: *For all who are led by the Spirit of God are children of God (8:14).* Being led by the Spirit is *not ... a spirit of slavery ... but ... a spirit of adoption (8:15).* Slavery involves fear but adoption offers trust.

(6) The witness of the Spirit: *When we cry, "Abba! Father!" it is that very Spirit bearing witness with our spirit that we are children of God (8:15-16).* Like Jesus, believers call God Father. *Abba* is the word for *Father* in Aramaic, the language of Jesus. When Jesus prayed to God, he spoke as a child to its father confidently and securely, reverently and obediently. When Paul prayed to God, he is doing the same. He is assuring his readers whenever they cry *Abba* they can be certain that they are really God's children. Moreover, they are not only children of God but also *heirs of God and joint heirs with Christ (8:17).*

(7) The first fruits of the Spirit: *We know that the whole creation has been groaning in labour pains until now; and not only the creation, but we ourselves, who have the first fruits of the Spirit, groan inwardly while we wait for adoption, the redemption of our bodies (8:22-23).* As the first fruits of the harvest were seen as a foretaste of the full harvest, so the Holy Spirit is seen as the anticipation of the ultimate salvation for

the creation and the creatures. *For in hope we were saved (8:24).*

(8) The intercession of the Spirit: *Likewise the Spirit helps us in our weakness ... that very Spirit intercedes with sighs too deep for words. And God ... knows what is the mind of the Spirit, because the Spirit intercedes for the saints according to the will of God (8:26-27).* We do not know what to pray for, what God's will is necessarily. But in and through *sighs too deep for words* the Spirit comes to the aid of our weakness. When we don't know how to pray in the face of human sickness, natural disaster, or evil activity the Spirit of Christ pleads for us in and through *sighs too deep for words.*

Part B Romans 8:28-39 presents a threefold message.

28 We know that all things work together for good for those who love God, who are called according to his purpose. 29 For those whom he foreknew he also predestined to be conformed to the image of his Son, in order that he might be the firstborn within a large family. 30 And those whom he predestined he also called; and those whom he called he also justified; and those whom he justified he also glorified. 31 What then are we to say about these things? If God is for us, who is against us? 32 He who did not withhold his own Son, but gave him up for all of us, will he not with him also give us everything else? 33 Who will bring any charge against God's elect? It is God who justifies. 34 Who is to condemn? It is Christ Jesus, who died, yes, who was raised, who is at the right hand of God, who indeed intercedes for us. 35 Who will separate us from the love of Christ? Will hardship, or distress, or persecution, or famine, or nakedness, or peril, or sword? 36 As it is written, 'For your sake we are being killed all day long; we are accounted as sheep to be slaughtered.' 37 No, in all these things we are more than conquerors through him who loved us. 38 For I am convinced that neither death, nor life, nor angels, nor rulers, nor things present, nor things to come, nor powers, 39 nor height, nor depth, nor anything else in all creation, will be able to separate us from the love of God in Christ Jesus our Lord.

(1) Assurance

There are three ways of interpreting Romans 8:28a. **First**, if we follow the traditional reading in the NRSV, 'all things' is the subject of the verb. *We know that all things work together for good for those who love God.* **Second**, if we follow the marginal reading in the NRSV, 'God' is the subject and 'all things' is the object of the clause. *We know that God makes all things work together for good for those who love God.* **Third**, if we follow the translation in the Revised English Bible, 'he' is the subject and refers back to the Spirit in the previous verse. *In everything, as we know, he co-operates for good with those who love God.*

The reasoning behind accepting the second or third interpretation of Romans 8:28a is as follows. Things do not work themselves out but, left alone, they go wrong. Rather, if we love God and are receptive to his will, God and/or the Spirit of Christ, works with us in bringing about good. The good things are described in what follows, *to be conformed to the image of his Son*, being made in the likeness of Christ.

God is like a chess grandmaster who takes into account our good and bad choices in life and fits them together so that they make a meaningful pattern. In everything the Spirit of God co-operates for good with those who love God so that his purpose is fulfilled in his people being made in the likeness of Christ.

Paul then uses a sequence of verbs: *foreknew ... predestined ... called ... justified ... glorified (8:29-30).* He stresses the certainty of our salvation as he indicates the various stages of God's working in our lives. Paul's deterministic language is a way of expressing God's grace. Our relationship with God does not depend on our own doing but on God's. Our assurance rests in God's purpose. Divine sovereignty and human responsibility interact in the mystery of God's choice.

(2) No condemnation

The cost of no condemnation is the death of Jesus and is reinforced as Paul parallels the offering of Jesus by God with the offering of Isaac by Abraham: *He who did not withhold his own Son, but gave him up for all of us (8:32)*. The story of Abraham includes these words: *By myself I have sworn, says the Lord: Because you have done this, and have not withheld your son, your only son, I will indeed bless you (Genesis 22:16-17)*.

The certainty of no condemnation is the resurrection of Jesus and is confirmed as Paul echoes the most quoted Old Testament passage: *It is Christ Jesus, who died, yes, who was raised, who is at the right hand of God (8:34)*. The songs of Israel include the oft quoted verse which was interpreted messianically: *The Lord says to my lord, 'Sit at my right hand until I make your enemies your footstool.'(Psalm 110:1)*

(3) No separation

Paul is not just a theoretical thinker; he is very practical: *Who will separate us from the love of Christ? Will hardship, or distress, or persecution, or famine, or nakedness, or peril, or sword? As it is written, "For your sake we are being killed all day long; we are accounted as sheep to be slaughtered." (8:35-36 quoting Psalm 44:22)*

Paul speaks from his experience of suffering which he shared with the Corinthians: ... *with far greater labours, far more imprisonments, with countless floggings, and often near death. Five times I have received from the Jews the forty lashes minus one. Three times I was beaten with rods. Once I received a stoning. Three times I was shipwrecked; for a night and a day I was adrift at sea; on frequent journeys, in danger from rivers, danger from bandits, danger from my own people, danger from Gentiles, danger in the city, danger in the wilderness, danger at sea, danger from false brothers and sisters; in toil and hardship, through many a sleepless night, hungry and thirsty, often without food, cold and naked (2 Corinthians 11:23-27).*

Even so, Paul writes to the Romans: *No, in all these things we are more than conquerors through him who loved us. For I am convinced that neither death, nor life ... nor anything else in all creation, will be able to separate us from the love of God in Christ Jesus our Lord (8:37-39).*

Finally, each chapter from 5 to 8 concludes with a focus on Jesus: *... just as sin exercised dominion in death, so grace might also exercise dominion through justification leading to eternal life through Jesus Christ our Lord (5:21).*
For the wages of sin is death, but the free gift of God is eternal life in Christ Jesus our Lord (6:23).
Thanks be to God through Jesus Christ our Lord!(7:25)
For I am convinced that neither death, nor life ... nor anything else in all creation, will be able to separate us from the love of God in Christ Jesus our Lord (8:38-39).

Prayer

Lord God, we thank you for the glad news of the Spirit instead of death. We seek to experience the law, mind-set, dwelling, life, leading, witness, first fruits, and intercession of the Spirit of Jesus as we follow him day by day. We acknowledge that our relationship with you does not depend on our doing but on your grace through faith. Give us the assurance that you are working with us in bringing about good. We are thankful for no condemnation because of the crucified and risen Christ and no separation from your love in Christ. In his name we pray. Amen.

Discuss

1   What are ways in which we experience the Spirit of Jesus in daily life?
2   How do we counteract a sense of condemnation?
3   How do we develop a sense of no separation from God's love?

John Wesley's Story

A 35-year-old Church of England clergyman went very unwillingly to a meeting in Aldersgate Street London, on the night of May 24, 1738. He had been a missionary in Georgia. He was a conscientious seeker after truth but he was not happy. At the meeting John Wesley heard a reading from Martin Luther's introduction to Paul's letter to the Romans. In his diary, Wesley records what happened: 'About a quarter to nine, while he was describing the change which God works in the heart through faith in Christ, I felt my heart strangely warmed. I felt I did trust in Christ, Christ alone for salvation: And an assurance was given me, that he had taken away **my** sins, even **mine,** and saved **me** from the law of sin and death.' John Wesley had come to personal faith in Christ.

Subsequently, Wesley organised his followers to meet weekly, to pray, read the Bible, discuss their spiritual progress, and to collect money for charitable purposes. With such method in their meetings, his followers were called 'methodists.' The spirit of John Wesley is expressed in his exhortation: 'Do all the good you can, by all the means you can, in all the ways you can, in all the places you, at all the times you can, to all the people you can, as long as ever you can.' Furthermore, Wesley preached outside the bounds of the Church of England. He travelled 4,000 miles a year, and preached 40,000 sermons in his lifetime. His followers were organised into a 'connection' and societies were linked into 'circuits' with an 'annual conference.' The Methodist movement spread to North America and beyond. Eventually Methodism separated from the Church of England but John Wesley remained an Anglican until his death in 1791.

All You Need is Good News

*St Stephen's Gate
Jerusalem*

Third Major Section of the Letter

Dilemma: How is Paul's letter to the Romans good news to Jews and Gentiles ?

Romans 9:1-29 talks about the dilemma of past tragedy

1 I am speaking the truth in Christ—I am not lying; my conscience confirms it by the Holy Spirit— 2 I have great sorrow and unceasing anguish in my heart. 3 For I could wish that I myself were accursed and cut off from Christ for the sake of my own people, my kindred according to the flesh. 4 They are Israelites, and to them belong the adoption, the glory, the covenants, the giving of the law, the worship, and the promises; 5 to them belong the patriarchs, and from them, according to the flesh, comes the Messiah, who is over all, God blessed for ever. Amen. 6 It is not as though the word of God had failed. For not all Israelites truly belong to Israel, 7 and not all of Abraham's children are his true descendants; but 'It is through Isaac that descendants shall be named after you.' 8 This means that it is not the children of the flesh who are the children of God, but the children of the promise are counted as descendants. 9 For this is what the promise said, 'About this time I will return and Sarah shall have a son.' 10 Nor is that all; something similar happened to Rebecca when she had conceived children by one husband, our ancestor Isaac. 11 Even before they had been born or had done anything good or bad (so that God's purpose of election might continue, 12 not by works but by his call) she was told, 'The elder shall serve the younger.' 13 As it is written, 'I have loved Jacob, but I have hated Esau.' 14 What then are we to say? Is there injustice on God's part? By no means! 15 For he says to Moses, 'I will have mercy on whom I have mercy, and I will have compassion on whom I have compassion. 16 So it depends not on human will or exertion, but on God who shows mercy. 17 For the scripture says to Pharaoh, 'I have raised you up for the very purpose of showing my power in you, so that my name may be proclaimed in all the earth.' 18 So then he has mercy on whomsoever he chooses, and he hardens the heart of whomsoever he chooses. 19 You will say to me then, 'Why then does he still find fault? For who can resist his will?' 20 But who indeed are you, a human being, to argue with God? Will what is moulded say to the one who moulds it, 'Why have you made me like this?' 21 Has the potter no right over the clay, to make out of the same lump one object for special use and another for ordinary use? 22 What if God, desiring to show his wrath and to make known his power, has endured with much patience the objects of wrath that are made for destruction; 23 and what if he has done so in order to make known the riches of his glory for the objects of mercy, which he has prepared beforehand for glory— 24 including us whom he has called, not from the Jews only but also from the Gentiles? 25 As indeed he says in Hosea, 'Those who were not my people I will call "my people", and her who was not beloved I will call "beloved". 26 'And in the very place where it was said to them, "You are not my people", there they shall be called children of the living God.' 27 And Isaiah cries out concerning Israel, 'Though the number of the children of Israel were like the sand of the sea, only a remnant of them will be saved; 28 for the Lord will execute his sentence on the earth quickly and decisively.' 29 And as Isaiah predicted, 'If the Lord of hosts had not left survivors to us, we would have fared like Sodom and been made like Gomorrah.'

Paul considers himself to be outside Judaism defined by the Pharisees, but inside Israel defined by the Christians. Accordingly, he faces a difficulty which is not easily resolved. Why have many of his own people, the Jews, rejected Jesus as the Messiah? Why have they apparently refused to accept God's mercy through faith in Christ?

Paul says, *I could wish that I myself were accursed and cut off from Christ for the sake of my own people (9:3).* In fact he is identifying with Moses who said after the incident of the golden calf, *But now, if you will only forgive their sin—but if not, blot me out of the book that you have written (Exodus 32:32).* Yet the ancient people of God *are Israelites, and to them belong the adoption, the glory, the covenants, the giving of the law, the worship, and the promises; to them belong the patriarchs, and from them, according to the flesh, comes the Messiah (9:4-5).* Furthermore, the divine existence of Christ is indicated by the description: *who is over all, God blessed forever. Amen (9:5).*

If the Jews have not all accepted Christ, has the promise of God failed? Paul answers this question emphatically and definitively. *It is not as though the word of God had failed (9:6).* Israel is not defined by physical descent or by works of law: *not all of Abraham's children are his true descendants ... not by works but by his [God's] call ... (9:7, 12)* The latter statement is part of Paul's argument which distinguishes the children of Isaac, Abraham's son, by asserting, *As it is written, 'I have loved Jacob, but I have hated Esau.' (9:13 compare Malachi 1:2-3)* Jacob represents the people of Israel.

If God preferred Jacob to Esau, Paul faces the question of God's justice. The quotation of Malachi 1:2-3 is explained when Paul quotes God's words to Moses *'I will have mercy on whom I have mercy ...'* and to Pharaoh *'I have raised you up for the very purpose of showing my power in you ...' (9:15, 17 compare Exodus 33:19; 9:16)* God remains the merciful and powerful sovereign.

The imagery of a potter leads him to understand God as the Creator and humans as his creatures: *Will what is moulded say to the one who moulds it, 'Why have you made me like this?' Has the potter no right over the clay, to make out of the same lump one object for special use and another for ordinary use? (9:20-21)* One is reminded of Jeremiah in the potter's house. *Then the word of the Lord came to me: Can I not do with you, O house of Israel, just as this potter has done? says the Lord. Just like the clay in the potter's hand, so are you in my hand, O house of Israel (Jeremiah 18:5-6).* Accordingly Paul says, *What if God ... has endured with much patience the objects of wrath that are made for destruction; and what if he has done so in order to make known the riches of his glory for the objects of mercy ... including us whom he has called, not from the Jews only but also from the Gentiles? (9:22-24)*

Noting that the objects of mercy are both Jew and Gentile, Paul quotes Hosea, *'Those who were not my people I will call "my people", and her who was not beloved I will call "beloved".' 'And in the very place where it was said to them, "You are not my people", there they shall be called children of the living God.'* (9:25-26 compare Hosea 2:23; 1:10) Indicating the identity of the true Israel, Paul quotes Isaiah, *'Though the number of the children of Israel were like the sand of the sea, only a remnant of them will be saved'* ... *'If the Lord of hosts had not left survivors to us, we would have fared like Sodom and been made like Gomorrah.'* (9:27-29 compare Isaiah 10:22-23; 1:9)

In this section Paul has spoken of God's sovereign freedom to deal with Israel and the nations. God's call includes neither Jew alone nor Gentile alone. It embraces all who respond to God's call, whether they be Jew or Gentile. For Paul this was foreseen and spoken of long ago in the Old Testament.

There are cases of the unexpected convert. N. T. Wright in his learned Gifford Lectures, *History & Eschatology*, retells a story by a Roman Catholic Cardinal about three young boys in 1939 who played a trick on the local priest in the confessional. Two 'confessed' a variety of sins and then ran away. The third, a Jewish boy named Aaron Lustiger, also 'confessed' but the priest was able to give him a penance to do. The boy was told to walk up to the giant crucifix in the church, look at the figure on the cross, and say three times, 'Jesus, I know you died for me. But I don't give a damn.'

Aaron thought that this was an easy thing to do. He went up to the altar and shouted, 'Jesus I know you died for me. But I don't give a damn.' Then he did it a second time. When he tried to do it a third time he could not complete the statement. He left the church humbled. In August 1940 Aaron was baptised and took a new name 'Jean Marie'. The Cardinal concluded his story with the words, 'And that boy is standing here now, speaking to you.' The Jewish Cardinal was Archbishop of Paris from 1981 to 2005.

Prayer

Lord God, we are confronted with the mystery of acceptance and rejection of the good news of Jesus. This was seen by Paul in the first century and is seen by us in the twenty-first century. We acknowledge that this applies to nations and to individuals. Just as there was a difference between Israel and non Israel then, so there is a distinction between Church and non Church now. Deliver us from unthinking pride and grant us true humility. We pray in the name of Jesus who leads us to follow him all the days of our life. Amen.

Discuss

1 How was Paul (like Jesus) blessed to be a Jew?
2 What are ways in which we distinguish between nominal faith and genuine faith ?
3 How do we guarantee that our faith communities are based on grace rather than race?

*Model of Herod's Temple
Jerusalem*

All You Need is Good News

Romans 9:30-10:21 talks about the dilemma of present responsibility

30 What then are we to say? Gentiles, who did not strive for righteousness, have attained it, that is, righteousness through faith; 31 but Israel, who did strive for the righteousness that is based on the law, did not succeed in fulfilling that law. 32 Why not? Because they did not strive for it on the basis of faith, but as if it were based on works. They have stumbled over the stumbling-stone, 33 as it is written, 'See, I am laying in Zion a stone that will make people stumble, a rock that will make them fall, and whoever believes in him will not be put to shame.' 1 Brothers and sisters, my heart's desire and prayer to God for them is that they may be saved. 2 I can testify that they have a zeal for God, but it is not enlightened. 3 For, being ignorant of the righteousness that comes from God, and seeking to establish their own, they have not submitted to God's righteousness. 4 For Christ is the end of the law so that there may be righteousness for everyone who believes. 5 Moses writes concerning the righteousness that comes from the law, that 'the person who does these things will live by them.' 6 But the righteousness that comes from faith says, 'Do not say in your heart, "Who will ascend into heaven?"' (that is, to bring Christ down) 7 'or "Who will descend into the abyss?"' (that is, to bring Christ up from the dead). 8 But what does it say? 'The word is near you, on your lips and in your heart' (that is, the word of faith that we proclaim); 9 because if you confess with your lips that Jesus is Lord and believe in your heart that God raised him from the dead, you will be saved. 10 For one believes with the heart and so is justified, and one confesses with the mouth and so is saved. 11 The scripture says, 'No one who believes in him will be put to shame.' 12 For there is no distinction between Jew and Greek; the same Lord is Lord of all and is generous to all who call on him. 13 For, 'Everyone who calls on the name of the Lord shall be saved.' 14 But how are they to call on one in whom they have not believed? And how are they to believe in one of whom they have never heard? And how are they to hear without someone to proclaim him? 15 And how are they to proclaim him unless they are sent? As it is written, 'How beautiful are the feet of those who bring good news!' 16 But not all have obeyed the good news; for Isaiah says, 'Lord, who has believed our message?' 17 So faith comes from what is heard, and what is heard comes through the word of Christ. 18 But I ask, have they not heard? Indeed they have; for 'Their voice has gone out to all the earth, and their words to the ends of the world.' 19 Again I ask, did Israel not understand? First Moses says, 'I will make you jealous of those who are not a nation; with a foolish nation I will make you angry.' 20 Then Isaiah is so bold as to say, 'I have been found by those who did not seek me; I have shown myself to those who did not ask for me.' 21 But of Israel he says, 'All day long I have held out my hands to a disobedient and contrary people.'

As Paul begins to discuss present responsibility he contrasts Gentiles who were not striving after righteousness yet found it *through faith (9:30)* with Israelites who were striving for righteousness *based on law (9:31)* but did not find it. Why was this so? *Because they did not strive for it on the basis of faith, but as if it were based on works (9:32).* Whereas the Gentiles can offer the obedience of faith, the Israelites understood obedience to the law in terms of specific acts of obedience such as practising circumcision, observing the sabbath, keeping the food laws, and isolating from Gentiles. Indeed, this means that they *have stumbled over the stumbling stone, as it is written, 'See, I am laying in Zion a stone that will make people stumble, a rock that will make them fall, and whoever believes in him will not be put to shame.'(9:32-33 quoting Isaiah 28:16)*

Paul is still wanting his fellow Jews to find salvation but he decries their ignorance of true righteousness as they are *seeking to establish their own (10:3)*. He urges them to heed his plea. *For Christ is the end of the law so that there may be righteousness for everyone who believes (10:4)*. Does this indicate that Christ is the termination/cessation or the goal/ outcome of the law? The former would mean that the old age of the law has given way to the new age of Christ. The latter would mean that the law has been fulfilled in Christ.

Thus interpretations range from Christ bringing the law to an end to Christ being the fulfilment of the promise of the law. The paraphrase of J. B. Phillips provokes thought: *For Christ means the end of the struggle for righteousness-by-the-Law for everyone who believes in him.*

First, the righteousness from the law is explained by an Old Testament quotation: *'the person who does these things will live by them.'(10:5 quoting Leviticus 18:5)* This is righteousness which is created and sustained by specific acts of practising circumcision, observing the sabbath, keeping the food laws, and isolating from Gentiles. Such righteousness identifies a relationship with God which is the special possession of the people of Israel.

Second, the righteousness from faith is explained by another Old Testament quotation: *Do not say in your heart, 'Who will ascend into heaven?'... or 'Who will descend into the abyss?' ... The word is near you, on your lips and in your heart ... (10:6-8 quoting Deuteronomy 30:11-14)* Paul's quotation is interspersed with references to Christ's incarnation, Christ's resurrection, and Christian proclamation. The focus of Leviticus 18 is on doing, whereas the focus of Deuteronomy 30 is on believing. On the one hand, Leviticus can be understood in terms of ethnic customs and ritual ordinances. On the other hand, Deuteronomy 30 can be understood in terms of the obedience of faith which responds to the gospel according to Paul.

Paul applies his reading of the Old Testament to his first century audience: *If you confess with your lips that Jesus is Lord and believe in your heart that God raised him from the dead, you will be saved. For one believes with the heart and so is justified, and one confesses with the mouth and so is saved. (10:9-10)* First century Christians expressed such belief with the heart and confession with the mouth in baptism. Then Paul continues to draw upon the Old Testament by quoting the same passage as he did in 9:33, *The scripture says, 'No one who believes in him will be put to shame.'(10:11 compare Isaiah 28:16)*

Paul stresses that the gospel speaks more universally than the law: *For there is no distinction between Jew and Greek; the same Lord is Lord of all and is generous to all who call on him. For, 'Everyone who calls on the name of the Lord shall be saved.'(10:12-13 compare Joel 2:32)* The words of Joel reinforce Paul's argument with unbelieving Jews. The good news is not confined to Israel, it is for Israel and the nations. So he proceeds to treat the proclamation of the gospel to Jew and Gentile.

Faith happens when people *call ... believe ... hear ... (10:14)* Proclamation takes place in accord with the Old Testament prophet: *'How beautiful are the feet of those who bring good news!'(10:15 compare Isaiah 52:7)* Unfortunately, once again in accord with the Old Testament prophet, *not all have obeyed the good news; for Isaiah says, 'Lord, who has believed our message?'(10:16 compare Isaiah 53:1)* In summing up Paul links faith and hearing with *the word of Christ (10:17)*, the preaching of the gospel.

After quoting from Psalm 19:4, Paul says of his fellow Jews, *Moses says, 'I will make you jealous of those who are not a nation; with a foolish nation I will make you angry.'(10:20 compare Deuteronomy 32:21)* He cites the Old Testament prophet about Gentile believers, *'I have been found by those who did not seek me; I have shown myself to those who did not ask for me'* and about Jewish nonbelievers, *'All day long I have held out my hands to a disobedient and contrary people.'(10:20-21 compare Isaiah 65:1-2)* So Paul concludes by underlining the dilemma of Israel's present rejection of God's way of righting wrong in Christ.

In this section Paul has spoken of Israel's freedom and responsibility in rejecting God's way of righting wrong.

Prayer

Lord God, we acknowledge you as the Creator and Redeemer of all. The diversity of people in terms of race, society, and gender remind us of Paul's words: *There is no longer Jew or Greek, there is no longer slave or free, there is no longer male and female; for all of you are one in Christ Jesus (Galatians 3:28).* Teach us how to relate to others in such a way that we avoid the exclusion of others on the basis of racial, social, or sexual differences. Let our church community be known for its right standing with you and right living by your standards. In Jesus' name we pray. Amen.

Discuss

1 How does Paul approach the question of divine sovereignty and human freedom?
2 How do we preach the gospel today in word and deed?
3 What are ways in which we can foster a multi-racial church community?

All You Need is Good News

*The Western Wall
Jerusalem*

Romans 11:1-36 talks about the dilemma of future mystery

*1 I ask, then, has God rejected his people? By no means! I myself am an Israelite, a descendant of Abraham, a member of the tribe of Benjamin. 2 God has not rejected his people whom he foreknew. Do you not know what the scripture says of Elijah, how he pleads with God against Israel? 3 'Lord, they have killed your prophets, they have demolished your altars; I alone am left, and they are seeking my life.' 4 But what is the divine reply to him? 'I have kept for myself seven thousand who have not bowed the knee to Baal.' 5 So too at the present time there is a remnant, chosen by grace.
6 But if it is by grace, it is no longer on the basis of works, otherwise grace would no longer be grace. 7 What then? Israel failed to obtain what it was seeking. The elect obtained it, but the rest were hardened, 8 as it is written, 'God gave them a sluggish spirit, eyes that would not see and ears that would not hear down to this very day.' 9 And David says, 'Let their table become a snare and a trap, a stumbling-block and a retribution for them; 10 let their eyes be darkened so that they cannot see, and keep their backs for ever bent.' 11 So I ask, have they stumbled so as to fall? By no means! But through their stumbling salvation has come to the Gentiles, so as to make Israel jealous. 12 Now if their stumbling means riches for the world, and if their defeat means riches for Gentiles, how much more will their full inclusion mean! 13 Now I am speaking to you Gentiles. Inasmuch then as I am an apostle to the Gentiles, I glorify my ministry 14 in order to make my own people jealous, and thus save some of them. 15 For if their rejection is the reconciliation of the world, what will their acceptance be but life from the dead! 16 If the part of the dough offered as first fruits is holy, then the whole batch is holy; and if the root is holy, then the branches also are holy. 17 But if some of the branches were broken off, and you, a wild olive shoot, were grafted in their place to share the rich root of the olive tree, 18 do not vaunt yourselves over the branches. If you do vaunt yourselves, remember that it is not you that support the root, but the root that supports you. 19 You will say, 'Branches were broken off so that I might be grafted in.' 20 That is true. They were broken off because of their unbelief, but you stand only through faith. So do not become proud, but stand in awe. 21 For if God did not spare the natural branches, perhaps he will not spare you. 22 Note then the kindness and the severity of God: severity towards those who have fallen, but God's kindness towards you, provided you continue in his kindness; otherwise you also will be cut off. 23 And even those of Israel, if they do not persist in unbelief, will be grafted in, for God has the power to graft them in again. 24 For if you have been cut from what is by nature a wild olive tree and grafted, contrary to nature, into a cultivated olive tree, how much more will these natural branches be grafted back into their own olive tree. 25 So that you may not claim to be wiser than you are, brothers*

and sisters, I want you to understand this mystery: a hardening has come upon part of Israel, until the full number of the Gentiles has come in. 26 And so all Israel will be saved; as it is written, 'Out of Zion will come the Deliverer; he will banish ungodliness from Jacob.' 27 'And this is my covenant with them, when I take away their sins.' 28 As regards the gospel they are enemies of God for your sake; but as regards election they are beloved, for the sake of their ancestors; 29 for the gifts and the calling of God are irrevocable. 30 Just as you were once disobedient to God but have now received mercy because of their disobedience, 31 so they have now been disobedient in order that, by the mercy shown to you, they too may now receive mercy. 32 For God has imprisoned all in disobedience so that he may be merciful to all. 33 O the depth of the riches and wisdom and knowledge of God! How unsearchable are his judgements and how inscrutable his ways! 34 'For who has known the mind of the Lord? Or who has been his counsellor?' 35 'Or who has given a gift to him, to receive a gift in return?' 36 For from him and through him and to him are all things. To him be the glory for ever. Amen.

This chapter continues Paul's argument that God fulfils his promises to Jews and Gentiles in Jesus the Messiah and the Lord. In conclusion, Paul will say that many Jews, like many Gentiles, will come to faith and obedience by the mercy of God.

At first Paul asks if God has rejected his people and draws a parallel with Elijah who thought that he was an isolated figure. *Do you not know what the scripture says of Elijah, how he pleads with God against Israel? 'Lord, they have killed your prophets, they have demolished your altars; I alone am left, and they are seeking my life.' But what is the divine reply to him? 'I have kept for myself seven thousand who have not bowed the knee to Baal.' (11:2-4 compare 1 Kings 19:9-18)* The point of the contrast is about grace and works: *So too at the present time there is a remnant, chosen by* **grace**. *But if it is* by *grace*, it is no longer on the basis of works, otherwise *grace* would no longer be *grace* (11:5-6).

Then Paul describes two groups, the elect and the rest: *Israel failed to obtain what it was seeking. The elect obtained it, but the rest were hardened (11:7).* He supports his argument with references to the Old Testament (Deuteronomy 29:4; Isaiah 29:10; Psalm 69:22-23). Next he asks about the purpose of Israel's stumbling and gives an intriguing answer. *So I ask, have they stumbled so as to fall? By no means! But through their stumbling salvation has come to the Gentiles, so as to make Israel jealous (11:11).* Furthermore the sequel to the gospel's success among the Gentiles is spelled out. *For if their rejection is the reconciliation of the world, what will their acceptance be but life from the dead!(11:15)* One may ask what is meant by *life from the dead?* Is it a spiritual quickening of the nations or the resurrection at the end of the age?

Paul reminds the Gentiles: *But if some of the branches were broken off, and you, a wild olive shoot, were grafted in their place to share the rich root of the olive tree, do not boast over the branches. If you do boast, remember that it is not you that support the root, but the root that supports you (11:17-18).*

Both Jews and Gentiles are told of the two sides of God's dealings. *Note then the kindness and the severity of God: severity toward those who have fallen, but God's kindness toward you, provided you continue in his kindness; otherwise you also will be cut off (11:22).* Accordingly Paul's warning to all is *but you stand only through faith ... provided that you continue in his kindness ... (11:20, 22)*

The mystery is: *a hardening has come upon part of Israel, until the full number of the Gentiles has come in. And so all Israel will be saved; as it is written, 'Out of Zion will come the Deliverer; he will banish ungodliness from Jacob.' (11:25-26 compare Isaiah 59:20-21 and Jeremiah 31:31-34)*

The idea that *all Israel will be saved* raises three sets of questions. Who is all Israel? When does Israel get saved? How does Israel get saved? One needs the wisdom of Solomon to answer these questions! Sundry commentators have made valiant attempts to do so.

In simple terms one may conclude that all Israel are the chosen ones of Jews and Gentiles (rather than the chosen ones of Jews); that the time of Israel's salvation is in the history of the church's mission to the world (rather than in relation to the second coming of Christ); and that Israel is saved through faith in Jesus the Messiah (rather than through the first of the two covenants).

In support of these conclusions one may refer to Paul's words: *not all Israelites truly belong to Israel ... not from the Jews only but also from the Gentiles (Romans 9:9, 24)*; the words of Jesus: *the good news must first be proclaimed to all nations (Mark 13:10)*; and the words of Paul: *the gospel ... is the power of God for salvation to everyone who has faith, to the Jew first and also to the Greek ... in it the righteousness of God is revealed through faith for faith (Romans 1:16-17)*.

The two sides of God's dealings with all are explained: *Just as you* [Gentiles] *were once disobedient to God but have now received mercy because of their disobedience, so they* [Jews] have now been disobedient in order that, by the mercy shown to you, they too may now receive mercy. For God has imprisoned all in disobedience so that he may be merciful to all. (11:30-32) In this section Paul has spoken of the merciful conclusion to God's dealings with Israel and the nations.

Paul concludes his contemplation of the mysteries of history with a burst of praise to the all knowing and all powerful God. *For **from** him and **through** him and **to** him are all things. To him be the glory forever. Amen.(11:36)* The significance of ***from him***, ***through him***, and ***to him*** in this benediction is captured by the NEB: *Source, Guide, and Goal of all that is.*

At the end of Romans 11 we may ask what can be said by Christians about Jews, for Jews, and to Jews. Perhaps the following points are helpful.

When Christians talk about Jews, they celebrate the shared olive tree. *But if some of the branches were broken off, and you, a wild olive shoot, were grafted in their place to share the rich root of the olive tree, do not boast over the branches (11:17).*

When Christians talk for Jews, they speak up against anti-Semitism. *They are Israelites, and to them belong the adoption, the glory, the covenants, the giving of the law, the worship, and the promises (9:4).*

When Christians talk to Jews, they share that they have found their Messiah. In the Fourth Gospel Andrew, Philip, and Nathaniel called Jesus *the Messiah ... the one about whom Moses in the law and also the prophets wrote ...* and *the King* of Israel *(John 1:41, 45, 49)*. Likewise in Romans, Paul encourages Jew and Gentile with these words: *to them* [the Israelites] *belong the patriarchs, and from them, according to the flesh, comes the Messiah, who is over all, God blessed for ever (9:5)*.

We may also ask, How do we resolve the seeming differences between the emphases on God's sovereign election and human free will? Calvin thought that the sovereignty of God is paramount: 'Who can resist God's will?' Arminius thought that human responsibility is primary: 'Everyone who chooses to believe will be saved.' Some theologians are universalists. They have said that God's ultimate will is that all will be saved. Other theologians think that Paul is not discussing the issue. Paradoxically, Paul is saying that people do not believe because they cannot and do not believe because they will not. Then there are theologians who think that divine predestination is plural and human freedom is singular. In conclusion, some theologians ask, 'Have we confused a matter of temporal process with the matter of eternal destiny?' However, of one thing we can be sure, everyone does agree that believers are saved to serve.

Prayer

Lord God, we acknowledge you as Source, Guide, and Goal of all that is. We look back to you as Source, seek you as Guide in the present, and trust you as Goal in the future. We pray in accord with Reinhold Niebuhr, grant us the serenity to accept things we cannot change, the courage to change the things we can, and the wisdom to know the difference. In the name of Jesus. Amen.

Discuss

1 What do we think of Paul's use of the Old Testament stories?
2 How does Paul resolve the opposites of the kindness and severity of God?
3 What are ways in which Christians can engage in dialogue with Jews?

Karl Barth's Story

A 32-year-old Lutheran pastor and theologian finished writing an exposition of Paul's letter to the Romans in 1918. He had written his commentary during the First World War. From his pastorate in Switzerland Karl Barth watched Europe in the convulsions of deadly warfare. He realised that the idea of inevitable human progress was false. He found hope in his study of Paul. Barth said in his preface to his commentary on Romans: 'The reader will detect for himself that it has been written with a joyful sense of discovery. The mighty voice of Paul was new to me: and if to me, no doubt to many others also. And yet, now that my work is finished, I perceive that much remains which I have not yet heard ... ' A reviewer of Barth's commentary said that it fell like a bombshell on the theologians' playground.

Barth compared himself to a man who clutched in the dark at a rope for help but found that he had pulled on a bell-rope which made a sound fit to wake the dead. Accordingly Barth's contribution was to expose the weakness of the liberal theology of the day, to oppose the idolatry of the Nazis under Hitler, and to write his lengthy but incomplete *Church Dogmatics*. During his one visit to the United States in 1962 he was asked if he could summarise the essence of the countless number of words he had written. He replied, 'Jesus loves me this I know, for the Bible tells me so.' Karl Barth died in 1968. He was the dominant Christian thinker of the twentieth century.

All You Need is Good News

St Peter's Basilica
Rome

Fourth Major Section of the Letter

Fairy Tale: How is Paul's letter to the Romans news too good not to be true?

Paul writes about the 'fairy tale' of the good news of God in Romans 12:1-15:13. Paul has moved from the 'tragedy' of the sin of humanity, to the 'comedy' of the grace of God, to the 'dilemma' of the purposes of God, and to the 'fairy tale' of the Christian life. The fairy tale is the news which is too good not to be true. Unlike other fairy tales, this one is true.

Although the description of the fourth section of the Letter to Rome as 'fairy tale' may seem strange, I am using the description in terms of Buechner's analysis in *Telling the Truth: The Gospel as Tragedy, Comedy, and Fairy Tale*, 'the tale that is too good not to be true because to dismiss it as untrue is to dismiss along with it that catch of the breath, that beat and lifting of the heart near to or even accompanied by tears.' I trust that my readers' thinking will be stimulated to move beyond words of encouragement to deeds of faith, hope, and love.

Romans 12:1-21 talks about the fairy tale of the upward relation

1 I appeal to you therefore, brothers and sisters, by the mercies of God, to present your bodies as a living sacrifice, holy and acceptable to God, which is your spiritual worship. 2 Do not be conformed to this world, but be transformed by the renewing of your minds, so that you may discern what is the will of God—what is good and acceptable and perfect. 3 For by the grace given to me I say to everyone among you not to think of yourself more highly than you ought to think, but to think with sober judgement, each according to the measure of faith that God has assigned. 4 For as in one

body we have many members, and not all the members have the same function, 5 so we, who are many, are one body in Christ, and individually we are members one of another. 6 We have gifts that differ according to the grace given to us: prophecy, in proportion to faith; 7 ministry, in ministering; the teacher, in teaching; 8 the exhorter, in exhortation; the giver, in generosity; the leader, in diligence; the compassionate, in cheerfulness. 9 Let love be genuine; hate what is evil, hold fast to what is good; 10 love one another with mutual affection; outdo one another in showing honour. 11 Do not lag in zeal, be ardent in spirit, serve the Lord. 12 Rejoice in hope, be patient in suffering, persevere in prayer.
13 Contribute to the needs of the saints; extend hospitality to strangers. 14 Bless those who persecute you; bless and do not curse them. 15 Rejoice with those who rejoice, weep with those who weep. 16 Live in harmony with one another; do not be haughty, but associate with the lowly; do not claim to be wiser than you are. 17 Do not repay anyone evil for evil, but take thought for what is noble in the sight of all. 18 If it is possible, so far as it depends on you, live peaceably with all. 19 Beloved, never yourselves, but leave room for the wrath of God; for it is written, 'Vengeance is mine, I will repay, says the Lord.' 20 No, 'if your enemies are hungry, feed them; if they are thirsty, give them something to drink; for by doing this you will heap burning coals on their heads.' 21 Do not be overcome by evil, but overcome evil with good.

At the beginning of this section the paraphrase of J. B. Phillips conveys the meaning of Paul's stirring call to commitment. *With eyes wide open to the mercies of God, I beg you, my brothers* [and sisters], *as an act of intelligent worship, to give him your bodies, as a living sacrifice, consecrated to him and acceptable by him. Don't let the world around you squeeze you into its own mould, but let God re-make you so that your whole attitude of mind is changed. Thus you will prove in practice that the will of God is good, acceptable to him and perfect. (12:1-2 Phillips)*

Paul is describing three elements of the Christian life: its dynamic or source of power (*the mercies of God*), its discipline or sense of dedication (*present your bodies as a living sacrifice*), and its destiny in the new age inaugurated by Christ (*be transformed by the renewing of your minds*).

Christians worship God by presenting their bodies *as a living sacrifice* and this is their *spiritual worship*. Christians are changed *by the renewing of your minds*. Paul in the first century is using cultic terms and giving them new definitions. The sacrifice acceptable to God is not a beast or a bird in the temple, but is the gift of one's body, mind, and spirit. That is to say, Christians in the twenty-first century worship God not just in church buildings for church services but in every day life. When followers of Jesus learn to trust and obey the Lord at home, work, and play they are offering what Paul calls *a living sacrifice*.

The Christians of Rome are urged *not to think of* themselves *more highly than* they *ought to think, but to think with sober judgement, each according to the measure of faith that God has assigned (12:3)*. Christians are *in one body* and have *many members*, but *not all the members have the same function (12:4)*. Examples of different gifts are seen in *prophecy ... ministry ... the teacher ... the exhorter ... the giver ... the leader ... the compassionate (12:6-8)*. Paul has given similar lists in 1 Corinthians 12:8-10 and Ephesians 4:11-12. The significance of the list in Romans is that it includes speaking and serving. God's grace is seen in words which speak from our mind and heart and in deeds which serve the needs of the last, the least, and the lost.

Paul sees genuine love in action. On the one hand, within the Christian house churches believers are urged to *hate what is evil, hold fast to what is good; love one another with mutual affection; outdo one another in showing honour. Do not lag in zeal, be ardent in spirit, serve the Lord. Rejoice in hope, be patient in suffering, persevere in prayer. Contribute to the needs of the saints; extend hospitality to strangers (12:9-13).* On the other hand, in relation to the external non-believing society believers are told: *Bless those who persecute you ... Rejoice with those who rejoice, weep with those who weep ... do not be haughty, but associate with the lowly; do not claim to be wiser than you are. Do not repay anyone evil for evil ... live peaceably with all. Beloved, never avenge yourselves ... Do not be overcome by evil, but overcome evil with good (12:14-19, 21).*

Against an unfriendly background, Paul draws upon Jesus' teaching (Matthew 5:44) and the Old Testament (Deuteronomy 32:35 and Proverbs 25:21-22): *Bless those who persecute you ... 'Vengeance is mine, I will repay, says the Lord.' ... 'if your enemies are hungry, feed them; if they are thirsty, give them something to drink; for by doing this you will heap burning coals on their heads.' (12:14, 19-20)*

The powerful motivation of the Christian pilgrim appears in five ways in the final section of Romans:
(1) the glow of the Spirit: *Do not lag in zeal, be ardent in spirit, serve the Lord (12:11).*
(2) the joy of the Spirit : *For the kingdom of God is not food and drink but righteousness and peace and joy in the Holy Spirit (14:17).*
(3) the power of the Spirit: *May the God of hope fill you with all joy and peace in believing, so that you may abound in hope by the power of the Holy Spirit ... by the power of*

signs and wonders, by the power of the Spirit of God (15:13, 19).
(4) the sanctification of the Spirit: *the offering of the Gentiles may be ... sanctified by the Holy Spirit (15:16).*
(5) the love of the Spirit: *I appeal to you, brothers and sisters, by our Lord Jesus Christ and by the love of the Spirit, to join me in earnest prayer to God on my behalf (15:30).*

Prayer

With eyes wide open to your mercies, Lord God, as an act of intelligent worship we give you our bodies, as a living sacrifice, consecrated to you and acceptable by you. Don't let the world around us squeeze us into its own mould, but we ask you to re-make us so that our whole attitude of mind is changed individually and corporately. We want to put into practice your good and acceptable and perfect will. Help us to appreciate differing ministries, to relate positively to others in the church, and to be effective witnesses for you in the world. In the name of Jesus. Amen.

Discuss

1   Do all Christians possess spiritual gifts?
2   What do we see as effective examples of Christian ministries today?
3   How does our relationship with God affect our relationships with other people?

All You Need is Good News

*View from the Dome of St Peter's Basilica
Rome*

All You Need is Good News

Romans 13:1-14 talks about the fairy tale of the outward relation

1 Let every person be subject to the governing authorities; for there is no authority except from God, and those authorities that exist have been instituted by God. 2 Therefore whoever resists authority resists what God has appointed, and those who resist will incur judgement. 3 For rulers are not a terror to good conduct, but to bad. Do you wish to have no fear of the authority? Then do what is good, and you will receive its approval; 4 for it is God's servant for your good. But if you do what is wrong, you should be afraid, for the authority does not bear the sword in vain! It is the servant of God to execute wrath on the wrongdoer. 5 Therefore one must be subject, not only because of wrath but also because of conscience. 6 For the same reason you also pay taxes, for the authorities are God's servants, busy with this very thing. 7 Pay to all what is due to them—taxes to whom taxes are due, revenue to whom revenue is due, respect to whom respect is due, honour to whom honour is due. 8 Owe no one anything, except to love one another; for the one who loves another has fulfilled the law. 9 The commandments, 'You shall not commit adultery; You shall not murder; You shall not steal; You shall not covet'; and any other commandment, are summed up in this word, 'Love your neighbour as yourself.' 10 Love does no wrong to a neighbour; therefore, love is the fulfilling of the law. 11 Besides this, you know what time it is, how it is now the moment for you to wake from sleep. For salvation is nearer to us now than when we became believers; 12 the night is far gone, the day is near. Let us then lay aside the works of darkness and put on the armour of light; 13 let us live honourably as in the day, not in revelling and drunkenness, not in debauchery and licentiousness, not in quarrelling and jealousy. 14 Instead, put on the Lord Jesus Christ, and make no provision for the flesh, to gratify its desires.

In the Roman Empire Christians spread the message on Roman roads, speak of Jesus in the Greek language, and to some extent live in a stable and peaceful environment. However, the Roman State has a totalitarian structure in which Caesar is in control of all. Accordingly, Jews and Christians have no say in government but, as Paul says, *Let every person be subject to the governing authorities; for there is no authority except from God, and those authorities that exist have been instituted by God (13:1).* He understands the relationship of the State to God in positive terms. *For rulers are not a terror to good conduct, but to bad (13:3).*

When Paul writes to the Romans, Nero has replaced Claudius as emperor but is not yet a persecutor of the followers of Jesus. So what is to happen when rulers are a terror to good conduct? Walter Shurden provides a helpful analysis from a Baptist perspective. In *The Baptist Identity* he discusses religious freedom with particular reference to the United States. He distinguishes different epochs. When Christians have not been endangered by the state, Baptists have been 'Romans 13 People' and have been appreciative of civil government. When Christians have lived and died in a time of persecution, Baptists have been 'Revelation 13 People' and have opposed the state. When Christians have been advised to render to Caesar the things that are Caesar's and to God the things that are God's, Baptists have been 'Matthew 22 People' and have legitimised but limit the state.

This means that Romans 13 must be interpreted in its context. There is a crucial element of difference between then and now. Paul understands civil government is under divine control: *there is no authority except from God ... Then do what is good, and you will receive its approval; for it is God's servant for your good. It is the servant of God to execute wrath on the wrongdoer (13:1, 3-4).* Paul speaks of a government worthy of civil obedience: *Pay to all what is due them—taxes to whom taxes are due, revenue to whom revenue is due, respect to whom respect is due, honour to whom honour is due (13:7).* The challenges facing Christians in an authoritarian state and in a democratic state may require differing approaches depending upon the ability of citizens to influence the policies and actions of the state.

Paul then turns from a believer's duty to the state to a believer's duty of love. *Owe no one anything, except to love one another; for the one who loves another has fulfilled the law (13:8).* He quotes four of the ten commandments, *'You shall not commit adultery; You shall not murder; You shall not steal; You shall not covet.'* These and any other *are summed up in this word, 'Love your neighbour as yourself.' Love does no wrong to a neighbour; therefore, love is the fulfilling of the law (13:9-10).*

One may well ask, 'How do you love your neighbour as yourself?' In *Beyond Words* Buechner puts it well, 'When Jesus said to love your neighbor, a lawyer who was present asked him to clarify what he meant by *neighbor*. He wanted a legal definition he could refer to in case the question of loving one ever happened to come up ... Instead, Jesus told the story of the Good Samaritan (Luke 10:25-37), the point of which seems to be that your neighbor is to be construed as meaning anybody who needs you. The lawyer's response is left unrecorded.'

At the end of chapter 13 Paul senses the 'already but not yet' of the transition from the old age to the new age. *Besides this, you know what time it is, how it is now the moment for you to wake from sleep. For salvation is nearer to us now than when we became believers; the night is far gone, the day is near (13:11-12).* He draws attention to the two ages: before the coming of Jesus the Messiah and after the crucifixion and resurrection of Jesus the Messiah. On the one hand, *the night is far gone*; on the other hand, *the day is near.* Accordingly, *Let* us then lay aside the works of darkness and put on the armour of light (13:12). That is to say, *not in revelling and drunkenness, not in debauchery and licentiousness, not in quarrelling and jealousy (13:13).*

Perhaps there are many congregations where the sins of revelling, drunkenness, debauchery, licentiousness are not known. However, the sins of quarrelling and jealousy may be too well known. The words of Paul are challenging: *Instead, put on the Lord Jesus Christ, and make no provision for the flesh, to gratify its desires (13:14).*

Prayer

Lord God, give us wisdom in the exercise of religious freedom: to render to Caesar the things that are Caesar's and to God the things that are God's; to be subject to the governing authorities whose rulers are not a terror to good conduct, but to bad; and to resist the idolisation of unjust, repressive, authoritarian, zealous, violent or unhinged leaders. Assist us to exercise thoughtfully our duty of love. Keep us from the sins of revelling, drunkenness, debauchery, licentiousness, quarrelling, and jealousy. Clothe us with the qualities of Christ our Saviour. In his name we pray. Amen.

Discuss

1 When are Christians to appreciate or oppose or legitimise the state?
2 What does it mean to love our neighbour as ourselves?
3 How do we take seriously the sins that really matter?

All You Need is Good News

Romans 14:1-15:13 talks about the fairy tale of the inward relation

1 Welcome those who are weak in faith, but not for the purpose of quarrelling over opinions. 2 Some believe in eating anything, while the weak eat only vegetables. 3 Those who eat must not despise those who abstain, and those who abstain must not pass judgement on those who eat; for God has welcomed them. 4 Who are you to pass judgement on servants of another? It is before their own lord that they stand or fall. And they will be upheld, for the Lord is able to make them stand. 5 Some judge one day to be better than another, while others judge all days to be alike. Let all be fully convinced in their own minds. 6 Those who observe the day, observe it in honour of the Lord. Also those who eat, eat in honour of the Lord, since they give thanks to God; while those who abstain, abstain in honour of the Lord and give thanks to God. 7 We do not live to ourselves, and we do not die to ourselves. 8 If we live, we live to the Lord, and if we die, we die to the Lord; so then, whether we live or whether we die, we are the Lord's. 9 For to this end Christ died and lived again, so that he might be Lord of both the dead and the living. 10 Why do you pass judgement on your brother or sister? Or you, why do you despise your brother or sister? For we will all stand before the judgement seat of God. 11 For it is written, 'As I live, says the Lord, every knee shall bow to me, and every tongue shall give praise to God.' 12 So then, each of us will be accountable to God. 13 Let us therefore no longer pass judgement on one another, but resolve instead never to put a stumbling-block or hindrance in the way of another. 14 I know and am persuaded in the Lord Jesus that nothing is unclean in itself; but it is unclean for anyone who thinks it unclean. 15 If your brother or sister is being injured by what you eat, you are no longer walking in love. Do not let what you eat cause the ruin of one for whom Christ died. 16 So do not let your good be spoken of as evil. 17 For the kingdom of God is not food and drink but righteousness and peace and joy in the Holy Spirit. 18 The one who thus serves Christ is acceptable to God and has human approval. 19 Let us then pursue what makes for peace and for mutual edification. 20 Do not, for the sake of food, destroy the work of God. Everything is indeed clean, but it is wrong for you to make others fall by what you eat; 21 it is good not to eat meat or drink wine or do anything that makes your brother or sister stumble. 22 The faith that you have, have as your own conviction before God. Blessed are those who have no reason to condemn themselves because of what they approve. 23 But those who have doubts are condemned if they eat, because they do not act from faith; for whatever does not proceed from faith is sin. 1 We who are strong ought to put up with the failings of the weak, and not to please ourselves. 2 Each of us must please our neighbour for the good purpose of building up the neighbour. 3 For Christ did not please himself; but, as it is written, 'The insults of those who insult you have fallen on me.' 4 For whatever was written in former days was written for our instruction, so that by steadfastness and by the encouragement of the scriptures we might have hope. 5 May the God of steadfastness and encouragement grant you to live in harmony with one another, in accordance with Christ Jesus, 6 so that together you may with one voice glorify the God and Father of our Lord Jesus Christ. 7 Welcome one another, therefore, just as Christ has welcomed you, for the glory of God. 8 For I tell you that Christ has become a servant of the circumcised on behalf of the truth of God in order that he might confirm the promises given to the patriarchs, 9 and in order that the Gentiles might glorify God for his mercy. As it is written, 'Therefore I will confess you among the Gentiles, and sing praises to your name'; 10 and again he says, 'Rejoice, O Gentiles, with his people'; 11 and again, 'Praise the Lord, all you Gentiles, and let all the peoples praise him'; 12 and again Isaiah says, 'The root of Jesse shall come, the one who rises to rule the Gentiles; in him the Gentiles shall hope.' 13 May the God of hope fill you with all joy and peace in believing, so that you may abound in hope by the power of the Holy Spirit.

Paul is concerned that trouble between Jews and Christians at Rome should not undo the unity of Jews and Gentiles in the house churches of the imperial capital. In AD 49, according to the Roman historian Suetonius, 'Claudius expelled the Jews from Rome since they had been continually causing disturbances at the instigation of a certain Chrestos.' This is probably a reference to disputes between Jews about Christ. After the death of Claudius in AD 54 it is understood that Jews, including Jewish Christians, returned to Rome.

Eight years before the writing of Romans, it is recorded by Luke that Paul met Aquila and Priscilla in Corinth *because Claudius had ordered all Jews to leave Rome (Acts 18:2).* So, when Paul writes to Rome from Corinth in AD 57 it is an open question how Jewish 'returners' would get on with Gentile 'remainers'.

The first half of chapter 14 deals with convictions of the so called weak Christians. The Jewish 'traditionalists' may be *the weak* who *eat only vegetables* and are told: *those who abstain must not pass judgement on those who eat (14:2-3)*. The Gentile 'liberals' may be those who *believe in eating anything* and are told: *Those who eat must not despise those who abstain (14:2-3)*.

Furthermore, *Some judge one day to be better than another, while others judge all days to be alike. Let all be fully convinced in their own minds. Those who observe the day, observe it in honour of the Lord. Also those who eat, eat in honour of the Lord, since they give thanks to God; while those who abstain, abstain in honour of the Lord and give thanks to God (14:5-6)*. It appears that two Christians can disagree and yet both can be right. The primary basis for Christian conduct and relationships is explained in the statements that *we are the Lord's* and that *each of us will be accountable to God (14:8, 12)*.

The second half of chapter 14 deals with attitudes of the so called strong Christians. The strong are instructed to treat the scruples of the weak with sensitivity: *Let us therefore no longer pass judgement on one another, but resolve instead never to put a stumbling block or hindrance in the way of another. I know and am persuaded in the Lord Jesus that nothing is unclean in itself; but it is unclean for anyone who thinks it unclean (14:13-14)*. All are reminded that *the kingdom of God is not food and drink but righteousness and peace and joy in the Holy Spirit (14:17)*. In particular, the strong are to use their liberty with the principle that *it is good not to ... do anything that makes your brother or sister stumble (14:21)*.

It is worth asking whether there are occasions when this principle of the weaker brother/sister does not apply. One may compare the situation in Paul's letter to Galatia when Paul opposed Peter in Antioch over the issue of table fellowship between Jews and Gentiles. *But when Cephas [Peter] came to Antioch, I opposed him to his face, because he stood self-condemned; for until certain people came from James, he used to eat with the Gentiles. But after they came, he drew back and kept himself separate for fear of the circumcision faction. And the other Jews joined him in this hypocrisy, so that even Barnabas was led astray by their hypocrisy. But when I saw that they were not acting consistently with the truth of the gospel, I said to Cephas before them all, 'If you, though a Jew, live like a Gentile and not like a Jew, how can you compel the Gentiles to live like Jews?'(Galatians 2:11-14)*

The first half of chapter 15 continues to deal with attitudes of the so called strong Christians by encouraging them to follow the example of Christ.

First, Paul writes of the pattern of love in Christ: *We who are strong ought to put up with the failings of the weak, and not to please ourselves. Each of us must please our neighbour for the good purpose of building up the neighbour. For Christ did not please himself ... Welcome one another, therefore, just as Christ has welcomed you, for the glory of God ... Christ has become a servant of the circumcised on behalf of the truth of God in order that he might confirm the promises given to the patriarchs, and in order that the Gentiles might glorify God for his mercy (15:1-3a, 7-9a).*

Second, he gives a proof from scripture: *'The insults of those who insult you have fallen on me.' For whatever was written in former days was written for our instruction, so that by steadfastness and by the encouragement of the scriptures we might have hope ... 'Therefore I will confess you among the Gentiles, and sing praises to your name' ... 'Rejoice, O Gentiles, with his people' ... 'Praise the Lord, all you Gentiles, and let all the peoples praise him' ... 'The root of Jesse shall come, the one who rises to rule the Gentiles; in him the Gentiles shall hope.'(15:3b-4, 9b-12)* The Old Testament quotations are from Psalm 69:9; Psalm 18:49; Deuteronomy 32:43; Psalm 117:1; Isaiah 11:10.

Third, he prays for unity and hope: *May the God of steadfastness and encouragement grant you to live in harmony with one another, in accordance with Christ Jesus ... May the God of hope fill you with all joy and peace in believing, so that you may abound in hope by the power of the Holy Spirit (15:5-6, 13).*

Throughout Romans Paul has quoted the Old Testament, especially the Book of Psalms. See 3:4 (Psalm 51:4); 3:10-12 (Psalm 14:1-3); 3:13a (Psalm 5:9); 3:13b (Psalm 140:3); 3:14 (Psalm 10:7); 3:18 (Psalm 36:1); 4:7-8 (Psalm 32:1-2); 8:36 (Psalm 44:22); 10:18 (Psalm 19:4); 11:9-10 (Psalm 69:22-23); 15:3 (Psalm 69:9); 15:9 (Psalm 18:49); 15:11 (Psalm 117:1). The Book of Psalms was the hymn book of the second temple.

Although Paul does not quote the well known Psalm 23 about the Divine Shepherd, it is worth retelling the following tale. The story of a famous orator giving readings which included Psalm 23 is found in various forms. The most recent retelling of this tale is by Fleming Rutledge in *The Expository Times*. She heard it in an Edinburgh chapel. Whichever version is told the gist of it is as follows. A famous orator was performing for an audience. He took requests for recitations of well known pieces of literature. One request was for the twenty-third Psalm, 'The Lord is my shepherd.' The orator agreed to recite the Psalm on the condition that the pastor making the request would do so after he had finished. The recitation proceeded professionally and effectively. The audience greeted the performance enthusiastically. Then the elderly pastor repeated the Psalm from memory. When he finished the audience sat in stunned silence. Someone asked the orator about the different reactions. He replied, 'I know the Psalm, but he knows the Shepherd.'

Prayer

Lord God, teach us to do three things. First, help us to follow the pattern of love in Christ who came not to be served but to serve and give his life as a ransom for all. Second, inspire us to search the scriptures of the Old and New Testaments to see the Bible as your single story as creator and sustainer, as saviour and redeemer, and as giver of life and meaning. Third, give us steadfastness and encouragement to live in harmony as followers of Jesus and to be filled with joy and peace in believing and to abound in hope by the power of your Spirit. In the name of Jesus we pray. Amen.

Discuss

1 How can we resolve differences between narrow minded and broad minded believers?
2 What does the Old Testament contribute to the gospel according to Paul?
3 Consider the precept of Peter Meiderlin:
    In essentials, unity;
    in non-essentials, liberty;
    in all things, charity.

David Suchet's Story

David Suchet has had a truly distinguished career on stage, in television and film. The actor is known for his portrayal of the Belgian detective, Hercule Poirot, in the television series based on the books of Agatha Christie. The fictional detective is always on the lookout for hard evidence. Suchet has presented television documentaries entitled 'In the Footsteps of St Paul' and 'In the Footsteps of St Peter'. Faith, it appears, plays a large part in his personal life. His autobiography *Behind the Lens: My Life* is well worth reading.

In fact, Suchet came to personal faith in 1986 at the age of forty. During the making of a film in Seattle, he had a moment of inspiration to start reading the letters of Paul from a Gideon Bible in his hotel room. He learned that salvation is offered through faith in Christ. By the end of the letters he found that he was reading about a way of being and a way of life that he had been looking for over many years. It was not until 2007 that Suchet made his faith public. Since then he has recorded the 66 books of the Bible from Genesis to Revelation in his deep and melodic voice. The set of five MP3 compact discs has been released by Hodder & Stoughton.

All You Need is Good News

Mosaic of Paul at Yalvac in Turkey

The Closing of the Letter

Romans 15:14-16:27 includes plans (15:14-33), greetings (16:1-23), praise (16:25-27).

14 I myself feel confident about you, my brothers and sisters, that you yourselves are full of goodness, filled with all knowledge, and able to instruct one another. 15 Nevertheless, on some points I have written to you rather boldly by way of reminder, because of the grace given me by God 16 to be a minister of Christ Jesus to the Gentiles in the priestly service of the gospel of God, so that the offering of the Gentiles may be acceptable, sanctified by the Holy Spirit. 17 In Christ Jesus, then, I have reason to boast of my work for God. 18 For I will not venture to speak of anything except what Christ has accomplished through me to win obedience from the Gentiles, by word and deed, 19 by the power of signs and wonders, by the power of the Spirit of God, so that from Jerusalem and as far around as Illyricum I have fully proclaimed the good news of Christ. 20 Thus I make it my ambition to proclaim the good news, not where Christ has already been named, so that I do not build on someone else's foundation, 21 but as it is written, 'Those who have never been told of him shall see, and those who have never heard of him shall understand.' 22 This is the reason that I have so often been hindered from coming to you. 23 But now, with no further place for me in these regions, I desire, as I have for many years, to come to you 24 when I go to Spain. For I do hope to see you on my journey and to be sent on by you, once I have enjoyed your company for a little while. 25 At present, however, I am going to Jerusalem in a ministry to the saints; 26 for Macedonia and Achaia have been pleased to share their resources with the poor among the saints at Jerusalem. 27 They were pleased to do this, and indeed they owe it to them; for if the Gentiles have come to share in their spiritual blessings, they ought also to be of service to them in material things. 28 So, when I have completed this, and have delivered to them what has been collected, I will set out by way of you to Spain; 29 and I know that when I come to you, I will come in the fullness of the blessing of Christ. 30 I appeal to you, brothers and sisters, by our Lord Jesus Christ and by the love of the Spirit, to join me in earnest prayer to God on my behalf, 31 that I may be rescued from the unbelievers in Judea, and that my ministry to Jerusalem may be acceptable to the saints, 32 so that by God's will I may come to you with joy and be refreshed in your company. 33 The God of peace be with all of you. Amen. 1 I commend to you our sister Phoebe, a deacon of the church at Cenchreae, 2 so that you may welcome her in the Lord as is fitting for the saints, and help her in whatever she may require from you, for she has been a benefactor of many and of myself as well. *3 Greet Prisca and Aquila, who work with me in Christ Jesus, 4 and who risked their necks for my life, to whom not only I give thanks, but also all the churches of the Gentiles. 5 Greet also the church in their house. Greet my beloved Epaenetus, who was the first convert in Asia for Christ. 6 Greet Mary, who has worked very hard among you. 7 Greet Andronicus and Junia, my relatives who were in prison with me; they are prominent among the apostles, and they were in Christ before I was. 8 Greet Ampliatus, my beloved in the Lord. 9 Greet Urbanus, our co-worker in Christ, and my beloved Stachys. 10 Greet Apelles, who is approved in Christ. Greet those who belong to the family of Aristobulus. 11 Greet my relative Herodion. Greet those in the Lord who belong to the family of Narcissus. 12 Greet those workers in the Lord, Tryphaena and Tryphosa. Greet the beloved Persis, who has worked hard in the Lord. 13 Greet Rufus, chosen in the Lord; and greet his mother—a mother to me also. 14 Greet Asyncritus, Phlegon, Hermes, Patrobas, Hermas, and the brothers and sisters who are with them. 15 Greet Philologus, Julia, Nereus and his sister, and Olympas, and all the saints who are with them. 16 Greet one another with a holy kiss. All the churches of Christ greet you. 17 I urge you, brothers and sisters, to keep an eye on those who cause dissensions and offences, in opposition to the teaching that you have learned; avoid them. 18 For such people do not serve our Lord Christ, but their own appetites, and by smooth talk and flattery they deceive the hearts of the simple-minded. 19 For while your obedience is known to all, so that I rejoice over you, I want you to be wise in what is good, and guileless in what is evil. 20 The God of peace will shortly crush Satan under your feet. The grace of our Lord Jesus Christ be with you. 21 Timothy, my co-worker, greets you; so do Lucius and Jason and Sosipater, my relatives. 22 I Tertius, the writer of this letter, greet you in the Lord. 23 Gaius, who is host to me and to the whole church, greets you. Erastus, the city treasurer, and our brother Quartus, greet you. 25 Now to God who is able to strengthen you according to my gospel and the proclamation of Jesus Christ, according to the revelation of the mystery that was kept secret for long ages 26 but is now disclosed, and through the prophetic writings is made known to all the Gentiles, according to the command of the eternal God, to bring about the obedience of faith— 27 to the only wise God, through Jesus Christ, to whom be the glory for ever! Amen.*

Plans

Paul considers his mission *to be a minister of Christ Jesus to the Gentiles in the priestly service of the gospel of God, so that the offering of the Gentiles may be acceptable, sanctified by the Holy Spirit (15:16).* Accordingly, his strategic plan has been, in his own words, *what Christ has accomplished through me to win obedience from the Gentiles, by word and deed, by the power of signs and wonders, by the power of the Spirit of God, so that from Jerusalem and as far around as Illyricum I have fully proclaimed the good news of Christ (15:18-19).* The primary reason for his visit to Rome is *to see you ... and to be sent on by you* [to Spain] ... *(15:24)*

In the meantime he says, *I am going to Jerusalem in a ministry to the saints; for Macedonia and Achaia have been pleased to share their resources with the poor among the saints at Jerusalem (15:25-26).* This collection for the Jerusalem believers is also mentioned in 2 Corinthians 8-9. (There may be an incidental reference to it in Acts 24:17.) Paul is aware of the perils of a Jerusalem visit and asks for prayer *that I may be rescued from the unbelievers in Judea, and that my ministry to Jerusalem may be acceptable to the saints (15:31).*

Greetings

As we noted in the background to Paul's letter to Rome, Paul is in Corinth when he writes. He mentions people in Corinth. *I commend to you our sister Phoebe, a deacon of the church at Cenchreae ... Gaius, who is host to me and to the whole church, greets you. Erastus, the city treasurer, and our brother Quartus, greet you (16:1,23).* The role of Phoebe is noteworthy. She is a deacon of the house church at Cenchreae which is a port of Corinth. Phoebe is the first person identified as deacon in Christian history. The mention of Erastus may also be significant. He is called the city treasurer. There is an inscription commemorating a person named Erastus at Corinth.

Although Paul is writing to Christians in Rome where he has not been, he has some friends there: *Greet Prisca and Aquila ... Greet also the church in their house. Greet my beloved Epaenetus ... Mary ... Andronicus and Junia ... Greet Ampliatus ... Urbanus ... and my beloved Stachys. Greet Apelles ... those who belong to the family of Aristobulus. Greet my relative Herodion ... those in the Lord who belong to the family of Narcissus ... those workers in the Lord, Tryphaena and Tryphosa ... the beloved Persis ... Rufus ...and ... his mother. Greet Asyncritus, Phlegon, Hermes, Patrobas, Hermas, and the brothers and sisters who are with them ... Philologus, Julia, Nereus and his sister, and Olympas, and all the saints who are with them (16:3-15).*

Prisca (Priscilla) and Aquila are known for their previous work as tent-makers with Paul in Corinth (Acts 18:2-3) and for their assisting Apollos by explaining the Christian way (Acts 18:26). Apparently they returned to Rome where they led a house church (16:5). Other household groupings appear in the families of Aristobulus (16:10) and Narcissus (16:11) as well as the two groups mentioned with Asyncritus (16:14) and Philologus (16:15).

Of particular importance is Paul's positive attitude to the ministry of women whose names are mentioned: Phoebe, Prisca, Mary, Junia [Joanna? Luke 8:3], Tryphaena, Tryphosa, Persis (16:1, 3, 6, 7, 12). Paul is notable for naming women as co-workers in various roles. In Roman society's patriarchal structure, he practised what he preached: *There is no longer*

Jew or Greek, there is no longer slave or free, there is no longer male and female; for all of you are one in Christ Jesus (Galatians 3:28).

Some opponents are described in broad terms: *I urge you, brothers and sisters, to keep an eye on those who cause dissensions and offences, in opposition to the teaching that you have learned; avoid them. For such people do not serve our Lord Christ, but their own appetites, and by smooth talk and flattery they deceive the hearts of the simple-minded (16:17-18).* We are unable to identify the opponents with certainty. Are they antinomian or gnostic or some other deviation? We don't know but Paul is sure that they shall not prevail. *The God of peace will shortly crush Satan under your feet (16:20).*

Benediction

By the end of his letter Paul's readers have become aware of the good news according to Paul.
First, in Romans 1:18-3:20, *the wrath of God is revealed from heaven against all ungodliness. and wickedness.*
Second, in Romans 3:21-8:39, *the gospel ... is the power of God for salvation to everyone who has faith ... For in it the righteousness of God is revealed through faith for faith.*
Third, in Romans 9:1-11:36, *the gospel ... is the power of God for salvation to everyone who has faith, to the Jew first and also to the Greek.*
Fourth, in Romans 12:1-15:13, *'The one who is righteous will live by faith.'*

The benediction sums up the themes of Paul's greatest letter:

*Now to **God** who is able to strengthen you according to my **gospel** and the proclamation of **Jesus Christ**, according to the revelation of the **mystery** that was kept secret for long ages but is now disclosed, and through the prophetic **writings** is made known to all the **Gentiles**, according to the command of the eternal God, to bring about the obedience of **faith**— to the only wise God, through Jesus Christ, to whom be the glory forever! Amen.(16:25-27)*

Prayer

Lord God, we pray that you will guide us as we make plans for living life in all its fullness. We pray too that we shall always be people who greet others positively and politely, with honesty and integrity. Finally, we pray that we may always offer you praise and thanksgiving as we cope with the mysteries of life and death. We pray to you the Triune God: Father, Son, and Holy Spirit; God for us, God with us, God in us; God everywhere, God there, God here. Amen.

Discuss

1   How do we make plans in the face of the uncertainties of life and death?
2   What are some practical ways of meeting and greeting others in a Christlike fashion?
3   Which themes of Paul's letter to Rome are relevant in the twenty-first century?

Appendix: The God of Jesus and Paul

WHO OR WHAT IS THE CHRISTIAN GOD?

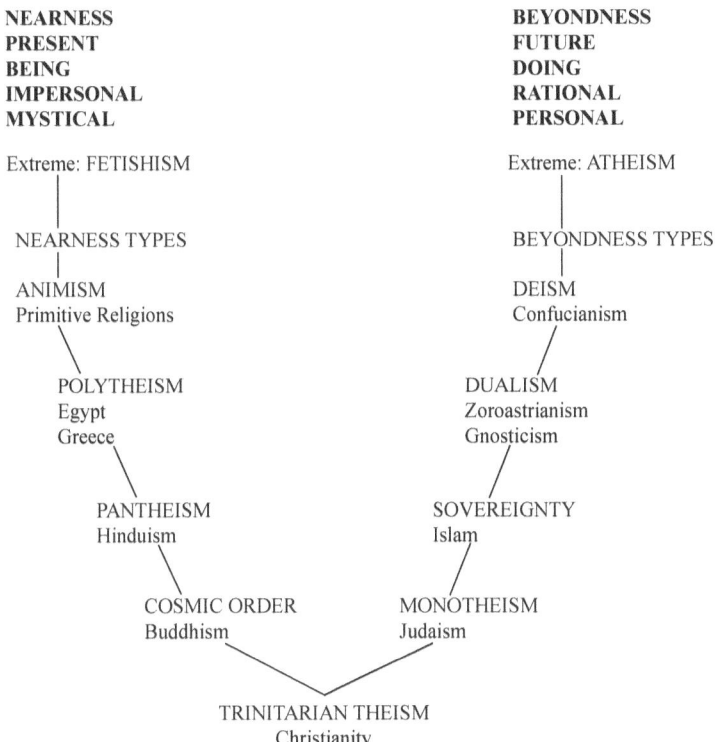

TYPES OF RELIGION
From a Christian perspective

NEARNESS	BEYONDNESS
PRESENT	FUTURE
BEING	DOING
IMPERSONAL	RATIONAL
MYSTICAL	PERSONAL

Extreme: FETISHISM — Extreme: ATHEISM

NEARNESS TYPES — BEYONDNESS TYPES

ANIMISM (Primitive Religions) — DEISM (Confucianism)

POLYTHEISM (Egypt, Greece) — DUALISM (Zoroastrianism, Gnosticism)

PANTHEISM (Hinduism) — SOVEREIGNTY (Islam)

COSMIC ORDER (Buddhism) — MONOTHEISM (Judaism)

TRINITARIAN THEISM
Christianity

GOD EVERYWHERE, GOD THERE, GOD HERE
GOD FOR US, GOD WITH US, GOD IN US.

Leon Morris has written, 'No book in Scripture is as God-centred as is this. Fundamentally Romans is a book about God.'

Accordingly, it is worth exploring different understandings of the divine. On the basis of the discussion by John Macquarrie in *Principles of Christian Theology*, I have adapted his diagram to portray such differences.

On the one hand, from the extreme of Fetishism (regarding an inanimate object with awe as having magical powers) there are Animism (believing that natural objects possess spirits), Polytheism (believing in many gods), Pantheism (identifying God or the gods with nature), Cosmic Order (identifying the divine with an impersonal order).

On the other hand, from the extreme of Atheism (not believing in the existence of God or the gods) there are Deism (believing in God who created the world but is now at a remote distance), Dualism (believing in two independent eternal principles: the one good, the other evil), Sovereign Monotheism (believing in the All-powerful One God), Personal Monotheism (believing in the Revelatory One God).

At the middle of the types is Immanent and Transcendent Theism (believing in the God who is near and far but reveals himself in person). This leads to Classic Trinitarianism, the God of Christianity.

A Christian follows Jesus according to the Gospels, the letters of Paul, the Acts of the Apostles, and the rest of the New Testament.

The Christian cannot accept a stark monotheism in which God is completely beyond, and even less an inclusive pantheism in which God is entirely near.

The Christian cannot accept a cosmic monism in which all differences are swallowed up in a divine unity, and still less a mythical polytheism in which there are all sorts of gods.

For the Christian, God is beyond and near, Creator not creature, Saviour not sinner, Revealer of light not darkness, Giver of life not death.

Paul died about AD 64. Jerusalem was destroyed in AD 70. The Arch of Titus in Rome was built by Domitian to celebrate the Roman defeat of the Jews in the revolt between 66 and 73 .

Afterword

By the end of Romans we have read Paul's version of the good news written from Corinth before his journey to Rome via Jerusalem. With inspiration from Frederick Buechner's analysis we have thought of Paul's good news as tragedy, comedy, dilemma, and fairy tale. Paul has expounded the tragedy of our sinfulness, the comedy of God's grace, the dilemma of rejection and acceptance of the Messiah, and the fairy tale of the divine transformation of human life.

Along the way we have marvelled at the impact of Romans on Aurelius Augustine in the fourth century, Martin Luther in the sixteenth century, John Wesley in the eighteenth century, Karl Barth in the twentieth century, and David Suchet into the twenty-first century.

It remains for us to continue reading Romans as a unique part of the Old and New Testaments. Paul challenges us to confront the tragedies of human existence, to see the unexpected action of the saving power of God in Christ, to struggle with the problem of differing responses of people to God, and to experience lives changed for the better in the fellowship of the Spirit of Christ.

When we read Paul's greatest letter with heart and mind, God our Father is able to keep filling us with joy and peace that comes from trusting in his Son Jesus, with the result that we overflow with hope by the Holy Spirit despite the ups and downs of life.

All You Need is Good News

Inside the Arch of Titus is a deep cut frieze of legions carrying treasures from the Temple after the Fall of Jerusalem in AD 70.

Select Bibliography

(1) Bible Translations

Barclay, William. *The New Testament* (Arthur James, 1988)
Bruce, F. F. *An Expanded Paraphrase of the Epistles of Paul* (Paternoster, 1965)
Good News Bible (The Bible Society in Australia, 1994²)
Holy Bible: New Revised Standard Version Anglicised Edition (SPCK, 2015)
Phillips, J. B. *The New Testament in Modern English* (Galahad Books, 1995)
The Holy Bible: New International Version Anglicised Edition (Hodder & Stoughton, 2011)
The Revised English Bible (Cambridge University Press, 1996)

(2) Background and introductory reading

Brown, Raymond E. *An Introduction to the New Testament* (Doubleday, 1997)
Bruce, F. F. *Paul Apostle of the Heart Set Free* (Eerdmans, 2000)
Davies, W. D. *Invitation to the New Testament* (Doubleday, 1966)
_____ *The New Creation* (Fortress, 1971)
Kümmel, Werner Georg. *Introduction to the New Testament* (Abingdon, 1975)
Moo, Douglas. 'Romans, Letter to the', *New Interpreter's Dictionary of the Bible*, 4:841-852 (Abingdon, 2009)
Polhill, John B. *Paul & His Letters* (Broadman & Holman, 1999)

Powell, Mark Alan. *Introducing the New Testament* (Baker Academic, 2018)
Review & Expositor vol. 73, no. 4 (Fall, 1976)
Review & Expositor vol. 100, no. 1 (Winter, 2003)

(3) Specially recommended for preaching and teaching

Barclay, William. *The Daily Study Bible: The Letter to Romans* (The Saint Andrew Press, 1975)
Barrett, C. K. *Reading through Romans* (SCM,1977)
Bird, Michael F. *The Story of God Bible Commentary: Romans* (Zondervan, 2016)
Buechner, Frederick. *Telling the Truth: The Gospel as Tragedy, Comedy, and Fairy Tale* (HarperSanFrancisco, 1977)
_____ *Beyond Words* (HarperSanFrancisco, 2004)
Cranfield, C. E. B. *Romans A Shorter Commentary* (Eerdmans, 1984)
Dunn, James D. G. *Romans: The People's Bible Commentary* (BRF, 2001)
Moody, Dale. 'Romans', *Broadman Bible Commentary*, 10:153-286 (Broadman, 1970)
Rutledge, Fleming. *Not Ashamed of the Gospel Sermons from Paul's Letter to the Romans* (Eerdmans, 2007)
_____ 'And finally … ' *The Expository Times* 116:396 (2005)
Witherington, Ben. *Paul's Letter to the Romans* (Eerdmans, 2004)
Wright, Tom. *Paul for Everyone: Romans Part 1: Chapters 1-8* (SPCK, 2004)
_____ *Paul for Everyone: Romans Part 2: Chapters 9-16* (SPCK, 2004)

Wright, N. T. and Michael F. Bird. *The New Testament in its World*, pp. 502-527 (SPCK, 2019)

(4) Advanced and detailed studies

Barrett, C. K. *Paul's Letter to the Romans* (Hendrickson, 1991²)
Cranfield, C. E. B. *The Epistle to the Romans*. 2 vols (T. & T. Clark, 1975-79)
Dodd, C. H. *The Epistle of Paul to the Romans* (Fontana Books, 1959)
Dunn, James D. G. *Unity and Diversity in the New Testament* (SCM, 1977)
_____ *Romans 1-8* and *Romans 9-16* (Word, 1988)
_____ *The Theology of Paul the Apostle* (Eerdmans, 1998)
_____ *Beginning from Jerusalem*, (Eerdmans, 2009)
Käsemann, Ernst. *Commentary on Romans* (Eerdmans, 1980)
Morris, Leon. *The Epistle to the Romans* (Eerdmans, 1988)
_____ 'The Theme of Romans', *Apostolic History & the Gospel*, pp. 249-263 (Paternoster, 1970)
Talbert, Charles H. *Romans* (Smyth & Helwys, 2002)
Wright, N. T. 'The Letter to the Romans', *New Interpreter's Bible*, 10:393-770 (Abingdon, 2002)
_____ *History & Eschatology* (SPCK, 2019)

(5) Miscellaneous Works

Jeremias, Joachim. *The Prayers of Jesus* (Fortress, 1978)
Macquarrie, John. *Principles of Christian Theology* Revised edition (SCM, 1977)
Moody, Dale. *Spirit of the Living God* (Westminster, 1968)

_____ *The Word of Truth* (Eerdmans, 1981)
Shurden, Walter B. *The Baptist Identity Four Fragile Freedoms* (Smyth & Helwys, 1993)
Suchet, David. *Behind the Lens: My Life* (Constable, 2019)

(6)   Reference Works

Bauer, Walter. *A Greek-English Lexicon of the New Testament and Other Early Christian Literature*
First edition, 1957, W. F. Arndt & F. W. Gingrich.
Second edition, 1979, F. W. Gingrich & F. W. Danker.
Third edition, 2000, Frederick William Danker.
(University of Chicago Press)
Macquarie Encyclopaedic Dictionary Signature edition (Australia's Heritage Publishing, 2011)

www.ingramcontent.com/pod-product-compliance
Lightning Source LLC
Chambersburg PA
CBHW030259010526
44107CB00053B/1767